The Tractor Trailer Book

Practical Advice For Driving
Tractor Trailers

Second Edition

Jimmy Cox

Disclaimer:
Some of the tips in this book describe how I deal with certain driving situations.
Traffic laws vary from state to state and every situation is different.
It is the readers sole responsibility to operate his or her vehicle in a safe manner.

About this edition

Since first writing The Tractor Trailer Book I've had many conversations on the internet with new drivers and I've received many comments and suggestions. I realized that there were many areas that I hadn't covered in the first book. This edition is an attempt to deal with some of those concerns. I've added a chapter about the basics of backing up a tractor trailer and I've included a section of delivery examples on my job and how I deal with them. I also wanted to make this edition more visual, with more diagrams. I hope you find this edition interesting and helpful.

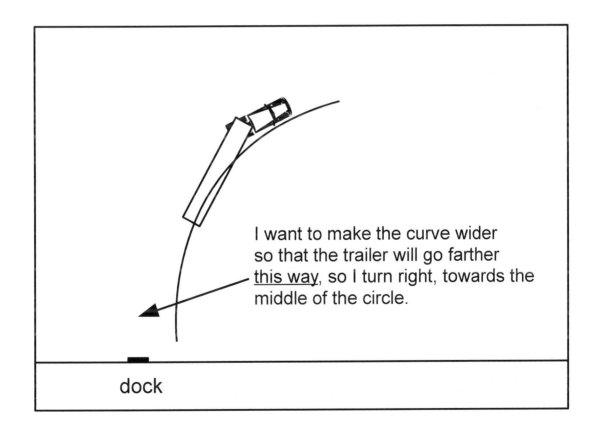

Some of the terms used in this edition

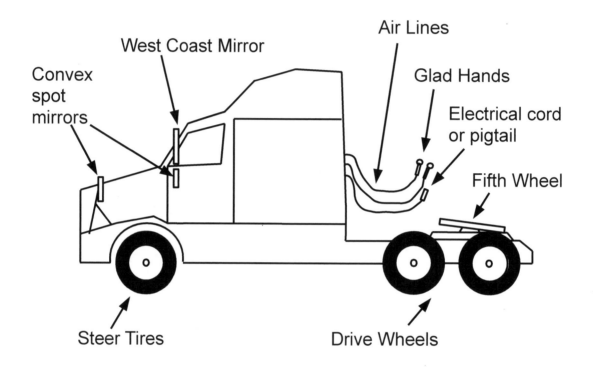

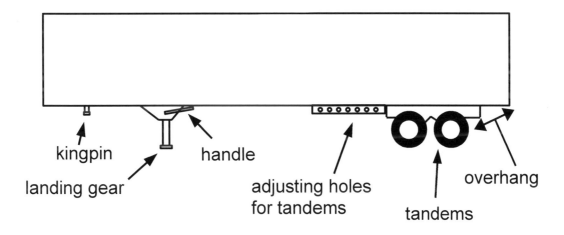

kingpin

landing gear

handle

adjusting holes
for tandems

tandems

overhang

To my wife, Nancy, and our family,
Ashley, Michael, Chloe, Mom and Dad,
and to my sister, Nancy, and her family

Contents

1

Know Where You're Going

I always feel bad when I hear a driver on the CB radio ask, "Does anybody out there know where XYZ company is located?", and no one answers. No one answers because the few drivers in the area that actually have their radios turned on don't know where XYZ company is located. Or maybe three drivers reply, each with their own idea of the best way to get there. It's up to the driver to decide which one to listen to. Either way it's not a good situation.

I had a job once delivering pizzas. I think it only lasted for a total of one week but I've always remembered what the owner of the pizza shop told me. He said that when I was making a delivery I should always know where I was going before leaving the restaurant. The same thing holds true for truck driving, but the consequences of getting lost with a truck can be far worse than delivering a cold pizza. You'll find that it's not very easy to turn a tractor trailer around when you miss your turn. In a small town you may have to go a mile or so before you can find a parking lot large enough to turn around. And attempting to go around the block in a city or residential area can make the problem worse. I missed a turn once trying to get to a company located near a residential section of Cleveland, Ohio. As I realized my mistake the streets were getting narrower and the side streets were so small that I couldn't turn into them to go around the block. I ended up having to back down two blocks until I found a side street wide enough to back into and get myself turned around in the other direction. There have been a couple times when I got lost and had the extra stress of finding myself facing a low bridge. There are few things more aggravating than coming up to a low bridge, having to back up into traffic, and then trying to find a way to make a U-turn. Even worse is when you find out that you were on the wrong street to begin with and that you didn't have to put yourself through all that aggravation.

Getting lost with a tractor trailer can greatly increase your chances of getting into an accident. You end up on streets where you shouldn't be driving. You become impatient because now you're late for your delivery appointment or behind whatever schedule that you had planned for the day, and when you get impatient and aggravated behind the wheel you can easily get into trouble.

So how do you prevent this? By doing whatever is necessary to know where you're going before you pick up your truck at the yard or before you climb out of your sleeper berth to get behind the wheel. With my present company I'm in a good situation as far as directions. I drive local delivery routes and I'm home every night. My company sends a message on the truck computer with all the stops for the following day. If I see a new location I ask them for the street address and then look it up on the computer when I get home.

But you may find, as I did at a previous job, that you don't know where you're going until you get to work that day. In that case you sit down and go through your stops and find them on a map. There's a temptation to just get in your truck and get moving but it's worth it to take the time to map out your route. Ask your boss about any stops that you're not sure of and ask him if any other drivers have been there before. Maybe you can reach the driver on the phone. If your company doesn't provide you with a road atlas it's worth it to buy one for yourself.

I've also been in the situation where you're out there on your own, over the road for days at a time, with a dispatcher giving you your stops over a computer in the truck. Many of these companies can send you directions over the computer that have been written out by other drivers. I always check my route on a map but I'll go with their directions if they've been written by another driver. Your route may look quicker but the other driver may know something that you don't, such as a low bridge, a one way street, or streets marked for no truck traffic. If it's a new customer it's possible that your company doesn't have directions yet. If you have a phone number on your paperwork try calling ahead for directions. If you have an early delivery for the following day, call early enough before everyone has left for the day and remind them that you're driving a truck. The directions may be different than those for a car.

If a delivery location becomes a regular stop on one of your routes don't assume that the way you got there is necessarily the best way. When you have time check maps of the area and watch for streets that may get you there easier. I've changed my routes sometimes after months of going to a location the same way. A different route may be quicker, or if not quicker, it may be easier on you and on the truck if there is less stop and go traffic. A different route may also be safer if the turns are easier and the streets less congested.

Know Where You're Going

At some point in time you may have to resort to getting on the CB to get directions. You may be an independent owner/operator with no support group that a company provides. If you've spent the night at a truck stop, get on the radio and ask for directions before you leave. You'll have more of a chance to get an answer and you won't have to be trying to drive while listening to directions. You'll find that the average CB radio only reaches out for two or three miles. If you reach someone while you're driving 65 miles an hour down the highway and they're going in the opposite direction at the same speed you'll only have a few seconds before they're out of range. Some drivers really get into spending time and money on setting up a CB radio. They purchase top of the line radios and have them tuned with custom antennas. I can't help you much there. I've had a $100 radio for about 8 years now and I usually only touch the volume and squelch knobs. The squelch knob is usually located to the right of the volume knob. It controls the distance of the signal that you're going to receive. When it's turned all the way to the left you'll hear a lot of static. That's also the position where you'll hear other radios at the furthest distance possible. To adjust it, gradually turn it to the right until the static disappears. Now you'll hear other radios at a moderate distance with no static. If it's some kind of emergency situation, bad weather perhaps, and you want to hear someone that's farther away from you, turn it to the left if you can stand the sound of the static. Only one person can talk at a time and that's determined by how close they are to you and the strength of their radio. Everyone else is drowned out. As I said, some drivers spend extra money getting a strong radio or having theirs beefed up by the local CB shop. If one of those drivers is at your truck stop and he feels like talking, singing, whistling, or playing his favorite song over the CB, good luck. You may have to wait awhile. That's why you use the radio for directions only as a last resort.

No amount of map checking will prepare you completely for a delivery if it's your first time to a location. There's usually something that can throw you off, such as a low hanging electrical wire for instance, or a fence or wall that's close to the dock. So before you leave, write down anything about that location that you'd like to remember for the next time when you go there. Don't leave and think that you'll have time to write it down later because chances are you'll forget about it. You may not return there for weeks or months so it will help if you keep notes, such as which side of the building the dock is located, or whether you need to back in from the street. I keep a folder of directions listed alphabetically by the name of the towns. You may want to arrange yours differently but I'd recommend that you write everything down. It makes life a lot easier when you have to return to a location that you haven't been to in a long time. Why spend so much time on directions? Because driving down the highway is easy. Getting in and out of a city or town to make a delivery is most of the battle. There are some more suggestions about directions in the city driving chapter. Just know for now that it's worth the time and effort to prepare yourself as much as possible so that you know exactly where you're going.

2

Make Sure That Everything Works

At the start of your work day your number one job is to make sure that everything on your tractor and trailer is working properly. When you start the engine on your tractor the oil pressure needle and voltmeter should come up immediately. Of course, the temperature gauges will take some time to come up to normal levels. If you use the same tractor all of the time, get familiar with the gauges so that you'll recognize when one of them is not at the usual reading.

Carry a working flashlight. You'll be checking things on your truck early in the morning or late at night when it's dark outside.

If you are waking up in your tractor with it already hooked to a trailer, part of your job is done. If you show up at a yard and have to hook up to a trailer, double check your paper-work and double check the trailer number to make sure that you're hooking up to the right trailer!

When it comes to hooking up to a trailer check the height of the trailer in relation to your 5th wheel. Someone with a tractor higher or lower than yours may have dropped it. One time I backed up to a trailer to hook up and it was so high that the 5th wheel actually ended up behind the pin. As you may know, the 5th wheel is balanced so that it tilts down toward the back when you're not hooked to a trailer. So when my 5th wheel went behind the pin, the front of the 5th wheel went back to the higher position making it impossible to pull forward without hitting the pin. I had to find a piece of wood to prop up the rear of the 5th wheel so that the front of it would clear the pin allowing me to pull out and start over after lowering the trailer. I also put a dent in the front side of a trailer one time trying to hook up to it when it was sitting too low. It had snowed heavily after the trailer had been dropped. Riding on top of the snow, I didn't realize that the tractor now was much higher than the trailer. So get out of your tractor and check the height, or if you have a day cab with a window in the back just swivel around to look before you back under it. If the trailer is sitting low, hopefully, you have a toggle switch to lower the air bags on your tractor. You can crank up a loaded trailer by hand as long as you've got the landing gear in low range, but it's not easy. However, if it's sitting too high it's usually not too hard to lower it by hand using the handle.

If you're trying to get your tractor under a trailer and your tires are spinning because of ice or snow remember to turn on your power diverter switch, if your tractor is so equipped, so that you engage more drive wheels. Just remember to turn it off when you're done. I've also used it many times when trying to back up to an inclined dock or parking lot during the winter. It doesn't hurt to carry a snow shovel and some rock salt to throw under the tires if you get stuck on ice or snow.

I'm writing this paragraph after having my feet go out from under me this morning at the yard where I pick up my truck. There was an icy spot on the asphalt that I didn't see. It happened so fast that it seemed that at one moment I was walking, and at the next I was hitting the pavement with my back and the back of my head. Oftentimes getting hurt on this job is just something as ordinary as falling down, whether walking on an icy parking lot or getting in or out of a tractor or trailer. Remember that in winter or rainy weather your shoes are going to be wet, so use both hands when climbing in or out of your tractor. Many trailers don't have steps or handrails so take your time getting in and out. Jumping out of a trailer to save a couple seconds can cost you weeks of being out of work. If there's ice on the parking lot, be careful if you're winding the trailer landing gear up or down, pulling the release handle, or getting up or down off of the catwalk to hook up your air lines. You don't want to be knocking yourself out cold in a dark parking lot in freezing weather with no one around to help.

If your tractor has been sitting unhooked and there is a lot of snow on the 5th wheel I always take a stick and brush it off the top and out of the slot for the kingpin so that the snow doesn't get packed in there and prevent it from locking.

You'll also find that the grease in the 5th wheel may get sticky in very low temperatures and will prevent it from locking all of the way. The first sign of this is that the release handle hasn't retracted all the way when you back into the pin. The first thing that I do after backing under the trailer is to get out with a flashlight and check that the trailer is sitting flat on the 5th wheel, and that the release handle has retracted. If the handle hasn't retracted all the way because of cold weather you usually can get it to lock all the way by using your clutch to gently rock the tractor back and forth against the pin.

I crouch under the trailer with a flashlight and check the kingpin lock every time that I hookup to a trailer. Maybe it's because of the time I dropped a trailer in the middle of a street by accident. When I worked in a shipping room, before I had a CDL license, I used to drive tractor trailers around the block from a parking lot to a garage so that we could load them. One time we had to switch tractors for one of the loads. We continued loading while one of the guys moved the tractors. I think that in an attempt to keep the trailer from jostling too much (we were still inside the trailer), he didn't back up hard enough into the pin. When it came time for me to move it out of the garage I figured that it was good to go and never bothered to check the hookup. I made it out of the garage ok, and even made the turn onto the street with no problem. But as soon as I straightened it out and gave it some power I felt the tractor shudder, saw one of the air lines in my mirror go flying up into the air, and heard a loud boom as the trailer hit the street. Because the landing gear had been raised, the front of the trailer was now so low that I couldn't get the tractor back under it. Thankfully, one of the guys in the company lumber yard saved me from having to crank it up by hand when he came out with a heavy duty fork truck and lifted the front of the trailer. I was able to lower the landing gear while he had it up in the air, then get under it again with the tractor. By this time, half of the people in the factory were at the windows wondering what was going on outside. Besides having to hear about it quite a few times afterward, I was called in on the carpet, as they say, to explain what happened to one of the big bosses. My boss backed me up, reminding him that I moved the trucks as a way to help out and that I didn't have a CDL license, (called a class one back then). It was one of those days that you'd like to forget but it made me aware of how important it is to check the hook up. It wasn't long after that happened that the company helped me get my license by letting me use one of the trucks for my road test. Figures 2-1 and 2-2 on the next page show the view of the backside of the fifth wheel and the trailer kingpin if you were crouched behind the tractor looking forward when it is under the trailer. If you check it every time you'll know what it looks like when it's locked. This way you'll immediately know when something looks different with the locking bar.

Fig. 2-1 Kingpin unlocked

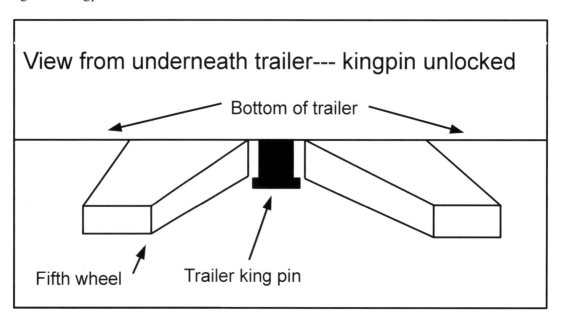

Fig. 2-2 Kingpin locked

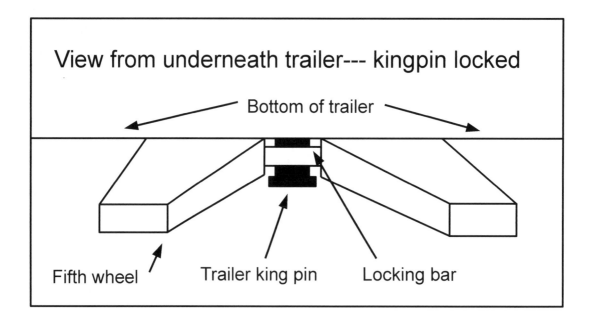

Part of your hookup procedure is to retract the landing gear. I do this right after checking the kingpin lock. Use low gear until most of the weight is transferred to the tractor. You'll know this when the handle begins to turn easier, then pull or push the handle shaft, (depending on your trailer), to get it into high gear to finish retracting the landing gear. I always raise them as far as possible. You never know when you might be going over a raised railroad crossing and you don't want to be catching them on anything. Don't forget to hang the handle on its holder so it's not swinging out into traffic.

The next thing that I do after hooking up to the trailer is to connect the air lines and the electrical cord. When I took my road test you were required to hook up your air lines after backing up your tractor so that it was just touching the trailer. For all I know, this may still be the required procedure. When hooking up to older trailers this was a way to provide air to the trailer so that you could set the trailer brakes before backing all the way under it. Modern trailers have brakes which set automatically when unhooked from the tractor and you'll see most drivers backing under the trailer first, then hooking up the lines. This has a couple advantages. In the winter, when the lines are stiff, they may not stretch all the way to an unhooked trailer without coming loose. Likewise, in the winter, you may need a little momentum to get under the trailer when the tractor wheels are on ice and snow. As you should know by now you have two brake lines, the emergency line and the service line. The air brake system on modern trucks is really an ingenious invention. Many people think that if an air line on a tractor trailer is accidentally cut, the truck has no brakes. Just the opposite is true. Someone realized that it would be very possible to lose air pressure because of an accident or a worn brake line, so they came up with the idea of spring brakes. The axles on the tractor and trailer are equipped with brake canisters that enclose powerful springs. The air pressure in the emergency line is actually used to hold back these springs. In the event of a loss of air pressure these springs push against a rod which applies the brake pads against the brake drums. When you apply your parking brakes at a delivery or at the end of the day, the air is released from the canister, allowing the springs to apply the brakes. So even if your truck loses air pressure after sitting overnight the springs prevent it from moving. Pay attention if you hear the warning buzzer come on and see your air pressure gauge dropping. The warning light and buzzer should come on if the air in the service reservoir has dropped to around 60 psi or less. Get off to the side of the road because when the air gets low enough, anywhere between 20 psi and 45 psi, the spring brakes will come on. The service brake line goes to a different system. This is air that applies the brakes when you are driving when you push down on the brake pedal. As you hook up your lines check the rubber grommets on the trailers connectors and the tractor connectors (or glad hands as they're called), for any cracks. These are meant to seal the connection when you hook up your lines. Theoretically, if you accidentally hook up your lines incorrectly on a trailer whose brakes are properly adjusted, you won't be able to move the trailer. If you've ever had your air lines disconnected while the tractor was running and pushed the red trailer brake valve in, the position for normal driving, you've noticed a stream of air coming out of the red emergency line. That's the supply of air that's necessary to keep your parking brakes off while you're driving. By crossing the lines the brake canisters won't be getting that supply of air, and your parking brakes will stay on. But if you're unfortunate enough to cross the lines on a trailer that has brakes that are out of adjustment, it might be possible to move the trailer, even though the brakes may be dragging. There have been occasions where drivers have done this, only to later realize that they've burned up the brakes on the trailer.

If you've hooked up to a trailer and pulled against the pin to check the hookup, you'll know if the trailer parking brakes are working. You should also check that the trailer service brakes, the ones you'll be using when you press the brake pedal, are working. To do this, push in the red and yellow brake buttons to release the brakes on both the tractor and trailer, then pull the trolley valve, sometimes called the hand brake. This is a handle usually labeled "not for parking", located on the steering column or dashboard. Now try to pull the trailer. If it doesn't move then you know that the service brakes are working. Push the handle back up and and if you're not leaving immediately reapply your parking brakes.

In this book I won't get into a complete checklist for your pre-trip inspection. But I suggest getting into the habit of walking around your truck and trailer and checking things like lights and tires in a certain order so that you won't miss anything. It can save you time by catching a potential problem early before it becomes a big problem later.

I pick up my trailer every morning in a lot where the trailers are in double rows, with the back door of my trailer about a foot or two away from the back door of a trailer in the second row. You may run into a similar situation at your lot or at a truck stop. And you may feel a little claustrophobic walking between them to check the rear trailer lights and door latches. I don't walk between them if there is a tractor hooked to the trailer behind mine and the engine is running. You're never sure what another driver might be doing. You can always move your trailer forward a little ways or to an open area after hooking to it and raising the landing gear to finish checking everything.

You'll see that most drivers kick their tires or use a thumper to check for any flats or soft tires. Remember that a flat tire won't look much different than the other tires because it's being held up by the other tires. You can use a gauge if you have time, but after kicking them often enough you can tell by the sound and the feel if one of them is soft.

If your trailer doesn't have a seal on the door and you have access to it, open the doors and make sure that the load is secured properly.

Make sure that the mirrors and windows are clean. You can get into trouble at the very beginning of your day by trying to pull out of a yard or parking space without being able to see clearly. If it's getting close to daylight you may think that it's not a problem if the mirrors are a little dirty but if the sun is behind you it reflects off of the dirt and greatly reduces visibility.

If another driver is having a problem with their truck at the yard or a truck stop be careful about helping them. Mechanics have a strict rule about not working on a truck unless the keys are removed because of a long history of people being killed or injured while working on a truck that was running.

So now you're satisfied that everything is working on your truck and you're ready to pull out of the yard or truck stop. It might be 4:00 in the morning and there may not be many lights on in the yard. Maybe it's raining. Turn down your dashboard instrument lights. The less glare that you have coming at you, the easier it is to see out into a dark yard where other drivers might be walking. You'll find that it also may help to lower your windows to see the mirrors if you have to maneuver around trucks to get out. Drive through the yard slowly, especially if you have to drive close to a row of trucks. A driver walking around his truck with the engine running may not hear you. Don't forget to buckle your seat belt. Besides saving your life in a crash, if you ever lose control and the cab is being shaken around, it will help keep you centered in the seat making it easier to regain control.

When it comes to getting in or out of a parking lot or yard, there is usually more than one way that you can maneuver your truck. Check all of the obstacles and think of all your options before moving in a small parking lot. Sometimes when you are in a hurry you think that the shortest way out is the quickest. It isn't if you have to stop to fill out an accident report. Figure 2-3 on the next page shows a situation that you may find in a truck stop. Taking a right out of this parking space is the shortest way out but it sets you up for three possibilities of hitting another truck, one with the tractor, and one on either side of the trailer. Taking a left out of the space will take a few extra seconds but there is much less chance of hitting something, especially if it's dark outside. If there's no room to circle around, (shown by the solid line), take the dotted line around the back of the row.

Fig. 2-3 The shortest way out isn't always the easiest. Taking a left out of this space may take a little longer but you have less chance of hitting anything.

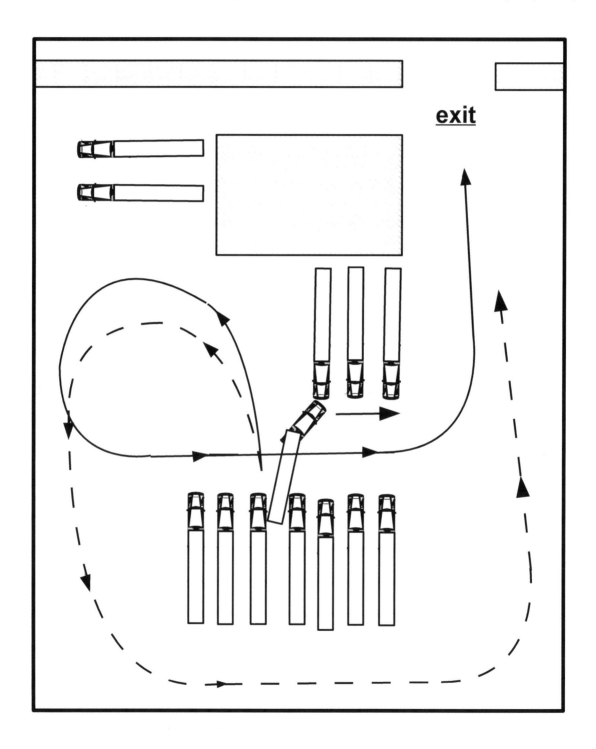

3

Shifting

Shifting the transmission on a tractor trailer is basically the same as that on a car, except that there are more gears and the clutch is harder to push. The truck I drive has a 10 speed transmission, probably the most common transmission on the road today, and it uses a split range device controlled by a small lever on the gear shift.

So instead of having 10 different positions, you shift through the first 5 gears with the range selector in the down position, pull up on the lever to put the transmission in high range, then go back and use the same sequence for the 5 higher gears. As you notice in figure 3-1, reverse has a low and high range, slow and fast. I don't think that I've ever used the high range in reverse. It's a good idea to go slow when in reverse, so low range has always been fast enough for me.

There are many different types of transmissions out there, too many to describe in this book. If you have access to a computer, there are some excellent driver forums where you could probably find information about the transmission in your truck.

Fig. 3-1. Shift Diagram (10 speed)

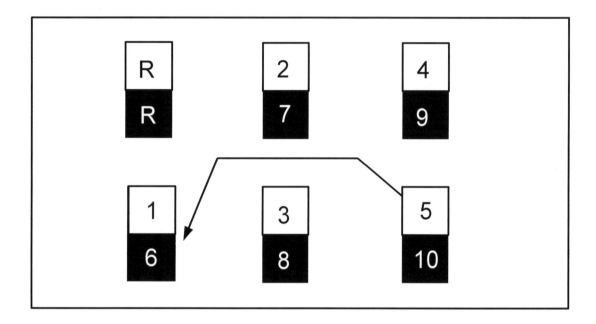

This is a typical shift pattern for a 10 speed transmission. The numbers on top of each other, for instance 1 over 6, don't mean that they are a different position. It's just a way to show them in a diagram. 1st is the same position of the shift lever as 6th. You don't have to work your way through the pattern every time. It's ok to skip a gear. For instance, if I'm on a slight downhill incline the truck will be picking up speed on its own, so I might go from 2nd to 4th. And you don't have to be in the 5/10 position to move the range lever up or down. If you're decelerating, you can go from 6th to 4th as long as your vehicle speed is slow enough for entering that gear.

Shifting

For now, as an example, I'll describe the procedure for my truck. After shifting into 1st, I slowly release the clutch, then push on the accelerator pedal. 1st gear on most trucks is geared so low that you don't have to hit the accelerator until after you've released the clutch. This saves wear and tear on the clutch. Then accelerate until the engine is up to a range of anywhere between 1300 and 1700 RPM. You'll find that you'll use that range differently, depending on conditions. If I'm on a level road and I want to conserve fuel I shift up at the lower end of that range, at around 1300 RPM. If you're going up an incline you may need to wind it out and wait until the engine speed is around 1700 RPM in order to shift smoothly. The engine spins so fast in 1st gear that it only takes one or two seconds to get up to the middle of that range, around 1500 RPM, then you'll need to shift into 2nd. Just like in a car, it takes a little longer in each gear for the engine to get up to optimum speed. So you'll only be in 2nd gear for a couple seconds before you reach 1500 RPM, then in 3rd gear for 2 or 3 seconds before you reach 1500 RPM, and so on. On the last shift you might be in 9th gear for about 10 seconds before shifting into 10th gear. This is assuming that you're on level ground. Of course, on any one of these gears, if you encounter an incline, you might have to stay in one of them longer in order to keep the engine at an optimum speed. If the incline starts getting steeper and the engine sounds like it's struggling, what's called lugging, shift down into the next lower gear, or however many gears, until you are at a gear where you can keep the engine in that area around 1500 RPM. When you are in 5th gear, and it looks like you'll have to keep shifting up, you pull the range lever up while you are still in 5th gear. When you push in the clutch and move the shift lever through the neutral area on the way to 6th gear, (same as 1st position), the transmission instantly shifts to the high range. Use the same procedure when shifting down. Push the range lever down while you are still in the higher gear. Then in the split second between shifts, the transmission goes into low range. If you accidentally push the range lever down while going along at 65 m.p.h. the transmission isn't going to suddenly put you into low range. Just flip the lever back up. It only changes the range when you take it out of gear and pass through the neutral area.

It doesn't hurt to stay in one gear for awhile. If I'm going through a town with a 30 mph speed limit I might be in 8th gear all the way through town.

Most transmissions are equipped with something called a clutch brake. It helps you get into gear when starting from a dead stop and it's activated by pushing the clutch all the way down to the floor. Once the truck has started moving you should not push the clutch down that far or you'll wear out the clutch brake. If the truck is in motion and you're using the clutch, pushing it halfway down is usually far enough.

There are different opinions about how to use the clutch. Many schools teach you to double clutch (push and release to take it out of gear, then push and release to put it into the next gear), because that's what many examiners want to see during your road test. After gaining some experience many drivers "float" the gears. This means shifting without using the clutch except for when you're starting from a dead stop. This is possible by getting the right combination of vehicle speed and engine speed. Personally, I always felt that it was awkward to pull it out of gear without using the clutch so I depress the clutch slightly to take it out of a gear and then slip it into the next gear without using the clutch. As I said, the engine speed to use as a guide for when to shift to the next higher gear on my truck is around 1500 RPM. When you back off on the accelerator to shift into the next higher gear the engine speed drops slightly. If you do this quickly enough, it won't drop more than one or two hundred RPM, (on my truck).

I use the same procedure only in reverse when down shifting. No matter what gear I'm in, if the truck has slowed down so that the engine speed is two or three hundred RPM slower than that optimum 1500 RPM speed, I take it out of gear, hit the accelerator quickly then immediately take my foot off the accelerator. This kicks the engine speed up two hundred or so RPMs and then I slip it into the lower gear as the RPMs are going back down..

After you become accustomed to shifting your truck you won't have to be watching the tachometer to know the best time to change gears. You'll know the best time to shift by listening to the engine. You'll automatically know which gear to select, depending on the situation, such as making a turn in city traffic. On my truck, if I have to slow down to make a typical left or right turn without coming to a stop, I usually have to drop down to 4th gear in the lower range. If it's an angle turn that I don't have to slow down as much as I would for a 90 degree turn, I can usually keep it in 6th in high range.

One driver asked about the speed range for each gear. Like I said, try to remember a good gear for doing typical things, like making a turn in an intersection. I'm including the approximate speeds for each gear in my 10 speed. You'll notice that the first couple gears are just to get the truck barely moving. You're not in them for very long and as you move up through the gears you stay in each one a little longer.

1st   gear- 0-2 mph
2nd gear- 2-4 mph
3rd gear- 4-7 mph
4th   gear- 7-10 mph
5th   gear- 10-15 mph
6th   gear- 15-20 mph
7th   gear- 20-25 mph
8th   gear- 25-35 mph
9th   gear- 35-50 mph
10th gear- 50+ mph

4

Highway Driving

As you pull out of the yard or truck stop, there's a good chance that you're going to make your way over to the nearest interstate highway. I mentioned in a previous chapter that driving down the highway is easy. Well, it's easy compared to getting around in city traffic, but it still has its own challenges that you need to think about.

When you get onto the highway you may have to go through a toll booth. You may have ez pass, as I do on my truck, which means you don't have to stop. There are certain areas where you need to be extra cautious. They include work zones, school zones, on and off ramps, and toll booths. As you approach a toll booth, stay off of your cell phone and the CB radio. On my truck, I know that if I'm in 4th gear and the engine is down to an idle, I know that I'm doing about 5 mph. If you know which gear will keep you down at that speed then you won't have to be looking down at the speedometer. The whole point of going slow through a toll booth is to be watching what's in front of you and paying attention. After you go through the toll booth watch both of your side mirrors as well as looking ahead. People in cars don't like getting behind a truck driver that has to accelerate through the gears and they'll come around you even when there's not enough room to safely do so.

As you enter an on ramp and prepare to merge onto a highway, check as soon as possible to see if there is an opening in traffic. Remember that it's not their responsibility to hit the brakes so you can enter the highway. In an ideal situation traffic would be able to move over to let you in but that's not always possible. If you have your CB radio on you may hear a driver telling you not to come out yet because there's traffic on their left side and they can't move over. So as you first enter the on ramp try to get an idea of how crowded the lane is and hopefully you can keep moving while picking a spot to enter the lane.

As you merge onto the highway, hopefully, you'll see cars and trucks moving over to let you in. Try to leave room in the merging lane to accelerate if you have to wait for an opening. After you've merged, cars can easily pass you and get back over to the right. Now, as you pick up speed, you may notice that the tractor trailer on your left that made room for you is going the same speed as your truck. Many companies limit the top speed on their trucks. Mine is set at 65. Some are set at 62. If I'm merging and the truck on my left can't get around me, I back off a little so that they can pass me and get back over to the right. They did me a favor by moving over to let me in. It's just common courtesy to let them get around you so they can return to the right lane. Nobody wants to be stuck out in the passing lane with traffic backing up behind them. If your truck is set faster than theirs you can always pass them once you get up to speed.

The main piece of advice I would give for highway driving is to look as far ahead as possible so that you can anticipate any problems. In a truck you sit quite a bit higher than in a car. Take advantage of that and pay attention to what's going on up ahead of you. During the winter when you have slippery road conditions leave extra space in front of you and if you see brake lights up ahead, start slowing down immediately instead of waiting until the last second. If you see a truck or car broken down on the shoulder move over, if possible, to give them some room. You may not realize until too late that they're not completely off of the road.

After you've been over the road for awhile you'll know which trucking companies are set at a slower speed than your truck. If you see one up ahead be ready to look for an opening to pass them.

You should always move over when possible to make room for law enforcement vehicles, emergency vehicles, or vehicles that are broken down on the shoulder. In many states it's the law.

Practice defensive driving just as you should when you drive your car. Defensive driving means that you should expect the unexpected, or expect the worst. If the car or truck ahead of you has to stop, for whatever reason, have you left enough room to stop before hitting them? Lets say that you're on a two lane road with traffic coming at you in the other lane and the car ahead of you signals to make a right hand turn. You don't want to lose your momentum so you keep going, assuming that they'll complete their turn and be out of your way. Now if they stop halfway through their turn, for whatever reason, you've left yourself no way out. You may hit them, or hit oncoming traffic, but you will hit something. Always assume that they won't complete the turn, and slow down enough to stop if necessary. Many people get impatient when they're around big trucks, so defensive driving means to be ready when they try to get around you at on ramps, at toll booths, or when you're trying to back up to a dock.

Highway Driving

When it comes to passing vehicles on the highway, you have to use your own judgment, your knowledge of your vehicle, and the weight of the load that you're pulling. Before you pass someone it's preferable to see if it's clear on your left side even before you signal. Check all of your left side mirrors before changing lanes, then check again as you move over (see fig.4-1). You'll be surprised at how many times cars try to get around you even after you've signaled and started moving over. Signal to return to the right lane as soon as possible and once again check all of your mirrors before moving over, and again as you move over. As a new driver, you'll find that it's a little scary moving back over to the right lane. The rear of your trailer is so far behind you that you're not sure if you've fully cleared the car or truck that you're passing. One rule is to wait until you see both headlights of the other vehicle in your big mirror. Until you get used to the distance in your mirrors you can also try moving your head over a little bit to the right. If your mirrors are adjusted properly, you should be able to get a little glimpse of the rear edge of your trailer. Also this is a time when many people driving cars try to get around your right side because they think you're taking too long to get back over. On my truck, as with most trucks, there is more of a blind spot on the right side than there is on the driver side. Get in the habit of sitting up a little higher when you check the right side mirrors. Think of it as a little stretching exercise. After all, you're sitting on your butt. A little exercise won't hurt. Most trucks these days have extra round spot mirrors on the front fenders, making it easier to see the blind spots next to your doors. If you don't have them on your truck, ask your company if they could have them installed, at least on the passenger side where you have the worst blind spot. They're not that expensive, much cheaper than the cost of an accident. If you see an uphill grade approaching and you're pulling a heavy load, it may not be a good time to pass someone. I've seen drivers ticketed for impeding traffic when they got out into the passing lane and traffic backs up behind them. If you're pulling a heavy load and come up to a steep hill, keep down shifting until you get to a gear that you can maintain a good engine speed. This might bring you down to 40 mph or less, so remember to switch on your emergency flashers. Also use your flashers when entering a highway when you can't get up to speed right away, such as when the entrance ramp is on a hill. Try to avoid passing another tractor trailer when traffic is merging onto the highway from the right side from on ramps and service areas. If you're about to pass another truck and you see traffic coming on from the right stay back and flash your lights so the driver knows that it's ok to move over. As you get close to the top of a hill you might come upon a truck going a little slower than you. At this point sometimes it's a good idea to back off a little instead of passing. You may find as you start down the hill that the other truck will be picking up speed very quickly. Once again you could be stuck out in the passing lane. Down shift early before going down a steep hill, especially if you see a slower speed limit coming up. It could mean that you're coming into a town or intersection. Using the engine brake can help slow you down and helps reduce wear on your brakes.

Fig. 4-1 Changing Lanes

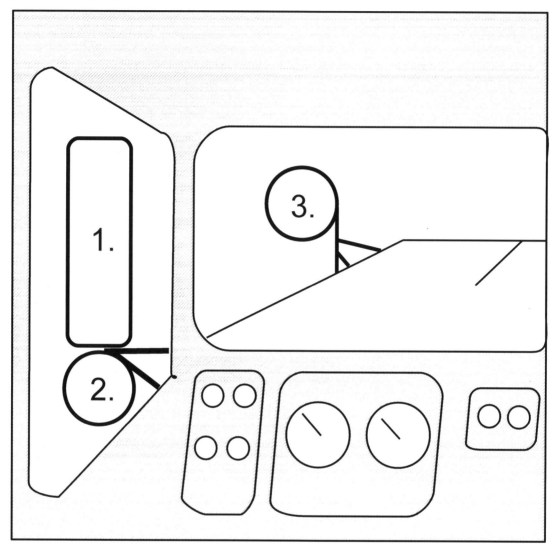

   Whenever I change lanes I check all three of my mirrors. You can use your own system but this is what I do. First I check the big mirror (west coast mirror) for a long view, to see if anyone in the next lane is coming up fast. If so I wait until they've passed. Then I check the big mirror again, drop down to the spot mirror to check for anything next to me, then the fender spot mirror to double check for anything close to me. Then I signal and start to move over. As I move over I repeat the sequence again, checking all mirrors. I repeat that sequence on the right side mirrors before signaling to move back to the right.

Speaking of making room for merging vehicles, recently I was driving on a highway and moved to the left to make room for a tractor trailer merging onto the highway from the right. There was a car behind the truck. As I was almost at the point of passing them the car moved over into the passing lane right in front of me, forcing me to hit the brakes. As I mentioned earlier, many people in cars don't want to be stuck behind a truck that is accelerating onto a highway and every now and then they'll do something stupid. So when you see a tractor trailer merging onto a highway with a car behind it, pay attention.

As for CB radios, they can be very useful or they can be a distraction. You'll find that other drivers will warn you about accidents up ahead, obstructions or debris in a lane, or broken down vehicles. Sometimes I think that it would be a good idea to have cars equipped with CB radios. It helps you to remember that you're dealing with a person, not just a vehicle. People seem less inclined to cut in line when they are in a bank or a store than when they are in a vehicle. Most people think that they are good drivers and overlook the times when they are being careless. Having someone in another vehicle letting you know what you're doing can be a good reminder. It's a good idea to have your CB on during bad weather. Other drivers will warn you about problems up ahead caused by the weather. I heard a couple drivers warn about ice one time while on a highway. I slowed down just in time. Even though I was driving slowly I felt my tires starting to slip. I pulled over at the next parking area along with some other drivers until the sand trucks came through. Just remember that the CB can also be a distraction. You should not be trying to give another driver directions while you are backing up to a dock or trying to maneuver in city traffic. The CB can be helpful in breaking up the monotony of a long trip. If you get talking to someone on a highway going the same direction as you are, such as another driver from your company, try not to tie up channel 19, the regular channel, for too long. One of you should suggest going to another channel. That way you'll leave channel 19 open for other drivers who are trying to get directions or trying to find out what's going on up ahead of them.

Here's a real basic question for new drivers. Are you keeping your truck in the middle of your lane? Check your mirrors to see if you have the same amount of room between your trailer and the right stripe and the middle stripe on the road. Once you have it in the middle, check to see how the front of the hood looks compared to the road. Try to keep it that way. After awhile you won't have to think about it. If one side of the back of your trailer is consistently too close to one of the lines then either your mirrors are out of adjustment or the trailer is "dog tracking", which means the axle is crooked and should be written up to be adjusted.

WINTER DRIVING

You should not use cruise control on the highway during slippery road conditions such as rain or snow. You don't want any delay in backing off the accelerator if you feel that you are losing control. You should also avoid using your engine brake on ice or snow. It can put too much braking action on your drive wheels, putting you into a skid.

In snowy weather the number one piece of advice is to slow down. You'll have more reaction time to correct any loss of control. Being able to see the pavement doesn't guarantee that the road isn't going to be slippery. Sometimes a light snow combined with just the right temperature can make the surface very slick. You should also try to avoid any sudden moves, either with your steering, or with the brakes or gas pedal. If I'm on the highway driving in snow and it looks as though I'll have to pass someone, I don't wait until the last minute. This gives me time to gradually move over to the passing lane. After making the pass I move back over to the right lane slowly. You may not notice this on dry pavement, but when you change lanes quickly there is a lot of sideways force on your tires, enough to make you lose control when you're driving in the snow.

You should also try to avoid making any sudden moves, either with the pedals or the steering while on a bridge in winter conditions. The cold air underneath the bridge makes any moisture on the bridge freeze quicker than other parts of the road. A driver that I worked with found this out first hand when he started losing it halfway across a bridge on the New York Thruway. By the time he got to the end of the bridge the truck was sliding out of control and he went down an embankment just past the bridge. The truck went on its side and he was banged up pretty badly. The only way he could get out of the cab was to kick out the windshield.

High winds can be as dangerous as snow or ice because your trailer acts like a sail, catching the wind and trying to push you. The combination of snow or ice plus high winds can be extra hazardous because now you've got the wind pushing you to the left or right and you have less traction to keep you from skidding to the left or right. If your trailer is empty you've got less weight pushing down on your tires so I slow down more when I'm empty. If you're driving a single axle tractor you've got even less tires on the road and less weight on the rear of your tractor, so you should slow down even more. I was driving through a snowstorm recently on a 65 mph highway and most of the traffic was going about 40 to 45 mph. Most of the pavement was snow covered. I was being passed by some trucks doing 50 mph but I assume that they had some weight on their trucks. I was empty so I kept it at around 40 mph.

In the case of ice on the road it's usually a good idea to pull over when safely possible and wait for the salt or sand trucks to come through. I ignored this piece of advice one time in Vermont when freezing rain had been coming down during the morning hours. A couple drivers on the CB radio going in the opposite direction warned me and another truck driver in front of me about some ice up ahead. Then I noticed that traffic up ahead had slowed to a crawl at a point where the road went down an incline. When it was my turn to go down the hill I saw that two cars had slid off the road at the bottom of the hill and there was a police car next to them with the emergency lights on. Even though it was only a two lane road there was probably enough room to pull off onto the shoulder which is what I should have done. I'm sure that by then the police had called for the salt truck so it probably wouldn't have been much of a wait. Seeing the truck ahead of me start down the hill, I thought that I'd try it as well, not realizing that maybe he had a lighter load on his truck while my trailer was fully loaded. (I said in the previous paragraph that it was preferable to be heavy for better traction, but going down an ice covered hill can change the rules). I thought that if I started slowly and kept the truck in a low gear I'd be ok. Halfway down the hill, with the weight of the load pushing me, I felt the drive wheels starting to slide and the truck started jackknifing to the right. By having the truck in a low gear, which is normally a good idea for going down a hill, it was like having the brakes applied just to the drive wheels while all of the other wheels turned freely. My first thought was that I was going to slide into the three cars at the bottom of the hill. Without thinking, I pushed in the clutch and took it out of gear. To my amazement the tractor and trailer straightened out. But now, I'm going down a hill in neutral which is a no no. I didn't worry about it too much because it was a short hill, about a quarter of a mile in length, but I should have left it in gear and just pushed the clutch in to stop the drive wheels from sliding. I lightly tapped on the brakes just enough to keep from hitting the truck in front of me and made it down the hill. If a similar situation came up again I would pull over to the side of the road.

Another problem associated with winter driving is fuel freeze up. Consider buying a container of diesel fuel supplement to add to your fuel tanks if it looks as if the temperature will be dropping. It may help prevent your fuel from freezing and shutting down the engine. I've had it happen more than once and it's no fun. You end up sitting on the side of the road with no heat (because the engine shuts down), and if it's cold enough to freeze your diesel fuel the cab is going to get cold quickly. When road service shows up they usually have to remove the fuel filter which is clogged with icy fuel. They empty it and refill it with new fuel, then add fuel supplement to your tanks. This problem occurs because all diesel fuel is not the same. Some truck stops winterize their fuel with additives, especially the ones in the northern areas of the country, while others may not. You can never be sure so it's a good idea to purchase a diesel supplement before you run into problems. Be especially aware of this if you've fueled in one of the southern states and are heading north into cold weather.

Be especially careful entering off ramps when you are driving on the highway during winter. They're narrower than the main road so they're more likely to be affected by blowing and drifting snow. You could be going 65 MPH down a clear road, then be looking at a snow covered ramp when you get off at an exit.

When driving on a highway, if you happen to miss your exit, resign yourself to the fact that you'll have to go to the next one and get back on the highway to go back to your exit. Do not attempt a u-turn across a median. It's dangerous enough for cars to do this, but even more so for a big truck. Because of the time that it takes to accelerate after coming to a stop, it is likely that you could cause an accident. Plus many median crossover strips are so narrow that you could get stuck halfway into a u-turn.

As you approach construction zones that reduce to one lane, watch for cars trying to get around you at the last minute. The closer that they are to you, the less likely you'll be able to see them.

Driving at night or in the early morning hours when it's still dark I have the dashboard lights turned down so that I'm just able to see the needles on the gauges. I don't know about your truck, but on mine the dash lights reflect off of the driver side window in the same area that I look through the window to see the spot mirror under the west coast mirror. It makes it look as though the dash lights are in the mirror. It would be easy to confuse a pair of headlights for the dash lights in the mirror.

You can help prevent fatigue when driving for a long stretch by sitting up straight. Keep your butt up against the back of the seat instead of slouching down. Your back will feel better, you'll have a better line of sight out of the mirrors, and it keeps you more alert.

If you see a sign that a weigh station or D.O.T. checkpoint is up ahead, it's a good idea to stay in the right hand lane. If those lights are flashing at the weigh station you have to pull in or take a chance of them coming out after you to give you a ticket with a hefty fine. Many states have permanent scale houses that weigh your truck as you drive through. My home state, New York, doesn't have many weigh stations but the D.O.T. sets up checkpoints in parking areas and toll road interchanges. As you drive through, if they stop you at all, it's usually just to ask where you're going, where you started from, and what you're carrying on the trailer. If they have you park your truck for an inspection and find any major safety problems, you'll be required to sit there until you have someone come to repair your truck. This is another reason to check your truck every day to make sure that everything is working properly. Besides checking lights, tires, air warning lights, and steering, they'll check for proper brake adjustment, and air lines that might be chafed from rubbing on the truck.

As you exit a highway you'll often come up to an intersection with a double turn lane, two lanes turning left, or two lanes turning right. I always try to be in the outside turn lane, (see figures 4-2 and 4-3). If I'm turning left, I stay in the right lane, and if I'm turning right, I stay in the left lane. When you're in the inside lane it's easy to lose sight of the cars in the outside lane when you start turning the tractor.

Fig. 4-2. Left hand turn (two left turn lanes)

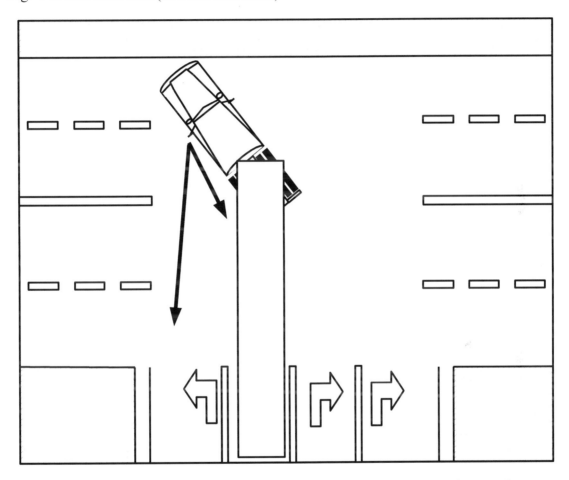

You'll notice in figure 4-2 that you have a good line of sight in your mirrors, (the approximate area shown by the arrows), when making a left turn from the right lane. You can see how close you are to any cars that might be turning along with you, and the only thing that you have to watch for on the right side is that you clear the right side curb or guardrail. If you were in the left lane, you'd have to watch the clearance on your left side for stopped traffic or a possible guardrail separating the lanes, while at the same time trying to see if anyone was coming around you on the right side, which will have a very limited line of sight.

Figure 4-3 shows a right turn with double lanes. Your line of sight in the right hand mirrors is not as good as when making a left turn, but if you are in the left lane there is much less to worry about. If you were in the right lane, you'd have to swing wide enough to clear the curb, while trying to look for cars coming around on your left side. Look at the right edge of your convex spot mirror to see the furthest area on your right.

Fig. 4-3. Right hand turn (two right turn lanes)

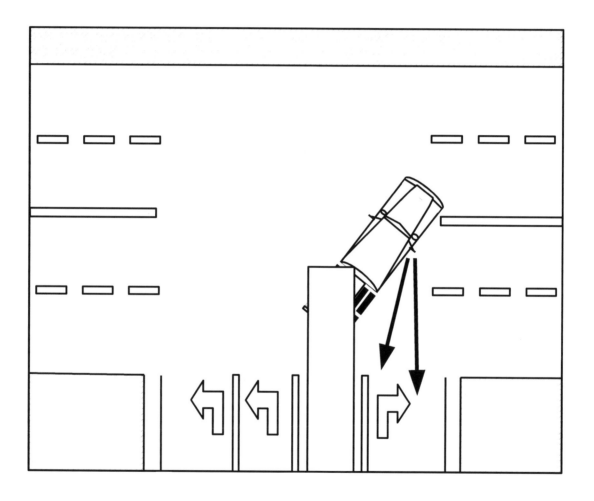

Slow down on the on and off ramps. Many truck loads are top heavy and can be easily tipped over. You'll see many skid marks and flattened guard rails on ramps where drivers failed to slow down. I'm very careful on off ramps, but on a couple occasions where I was distracted by merging traffic, I entered off ramps faster than I would like. Figure 4-4 shows what has worked for me. If you realize that you're going too fast into an off ramp stay away from the outside edge of the corner if possible. Most roadways slope down at the edge for drainage and the last thing that you want to be doing is tipping towards the outside of the curve. I steer towards the inside of the curve and do my heaviest braking while the tractor and trailer are still in a straight line. Of course, if there is a guard rail on the inside you have to avoid hitting it. There may not even be room to stay on the inside of the curve. The best way to get out of this situation is to not get into it. Be aware of when your exit is coming up so that you have time to slow down and try to be in the correct lane so that you don't have to speed up at the last minute in order to change lanes. This is another example of the importance of Chapter 1, Know Where You're Going. If your route involves having to take a number of exits, write the exit numbers down before you leave.

Fig. 4-4. Emergency braking at off ramp

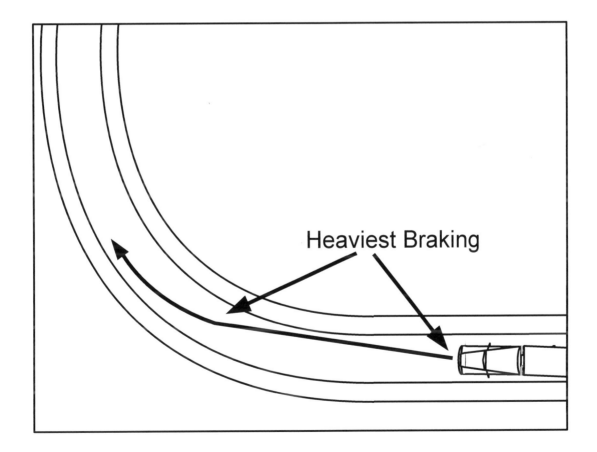

5

City Driving

Sometimes when I'm walking next to the tractor and the trailer I realize how big they are and it seems hard to believe that we can maneuver them through city streets. But you can do it as long as you take your time. When you pull off the highway to go into a city or a town you have to raise your level of awareness. Generally you'll be making more decisions in a short amount of time. Your job here will be easier if you've been able to make detailed directions. When you're figuring out how to get to a location in a city or town you should also figure out, ahead of time, how you're going to get out. What direction are you going to have to go when you leave your stop? What streets or route numbers do you have to follow to get you to the interstate that you need to be on for your next delivery? When you are entering a city or town, and you know that you'll be crossing one of your exit routes, look for it as you come into town.

You might be thinking now that you'll be trying to do two things at once. It's difficult enough just to find your delivery. But if you make note of your exit route while on the way in, it will be that much easier to find your way out. Make a note of any landmarks such as gas stations or restaurants on the corner of the street that you'll have to find on the way out. Is it a narrow street? You'll know that you have to move over before you get to the corner in order to make the turn. If you use a computer to see the delivery location, zoom in as much as possible. You'll see arrows if it's on a one way street. If so, obviously you won't be going out the same way you came in.

One of the biggest problems of city driving is making turns, especially if it's the first time to a delivery location. You may have to wait for traffic to move out of your way when making a tight turn, but just be patient. Most people aren't too keen on the idea of getting hit by a truck and will move out of your way if possible. In fact many times when turning, people on the street that I'm turning into will back up far more than necessary. I wave to them to tell them thanks, but also as a way to tell them that they don't have to back up any further.

If you know ahead of time when a turn is coming up you can prepare to move over first, if necessary, to make a wide turn. That's why directions are important. If you know the name of the street you're crossing before you get to your street, it gives you more of a warning. If you get a red light at that intersection and there is no one in front of you it's not a bad idea sometimes to stop a few feet before the stop mark or crosswalk. Then, when you get the green, you have a few extra feet to angle away from the curb, if necessary, in order to make a wide turn. It's also a good idea to stop before the stop line if you see that another tractor trailer is about to turn onto your street. Doing so leaves the other truck more room to make the turn.

If I'm making a right turn, the first thing that I watch for is to make sure that no one is trying to get around from behind the right side of my trailer (see figure 5-1). While checking that, I'm also checking that the left front of my tractor is going to clear cars on the street that are waiting at the red light or stop sign. Take it slow and check back and forth. After you're sure that no one is trying to come around the back side of your trailer, you now check your right side mirror to see if you're going to clear the curb, or light post, or whatever happens to be sticking out the furthest on the right hand corner. If you've judged it correctly you'll clear the turn. If it looks as though you're going to hit something with the right rear of your trailer don't continue so that you're almost up against it. You'll have to wait for the light to turn, or for the cars to the left of your tractor to move out of your way. Do not back up. At this point in your turn someone may be behind you and you would have no way of knowing. Once the traffic has moved, if you've left some room before coming up against whatever is near the right rear of your trailer, you can now turn the wheel to the left so that the tractor is at a straight line with the trailer and pull ahead to clear whatever was on the right side of the trailer.

As a rule, it's a good idea not to be more than 5 feet from the curb before making a right turn in order to discourage cars from coming up along the right side of your trailer. I have a couple locations where the entrance is so narrow that I have to be in the second lane over from the curb (two lanes in each direction), and even then the trailer wheels are going over the curb. Of course, you need to be extra cautious in a situation like this. If there is a lot of traffic, I'll pull over to the right side curb a couple hundred feet before the entrance with my emergency flashers on and wait for the traffic to clear. After it's clear I pull out to the left and then make the turn, alternately watching the right side of the trailer and the entrance. You can make it easier on yourself if you can approach the entrance from the other direction. You have more room making a left hand turn because you're further away from the curb, but if coming in from the other direction means going around a lot of narrow city intersections it won't be making it much safer.

Fig. 5-1. Right turn

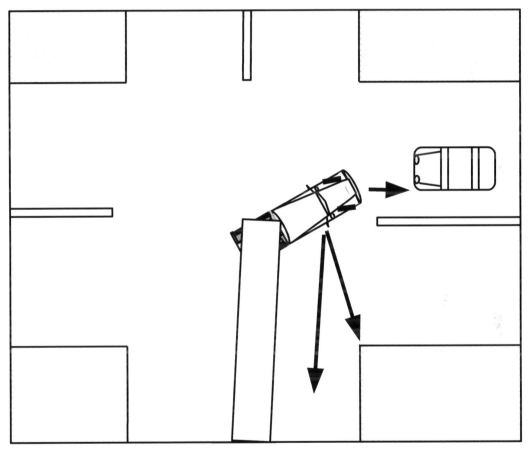

Figure 5-1 shows a right turn on narrow city streets. The arrows show where you should be looking. Check back and forth as you slowly make the turn to see the clearance from the front of your tractor to the car, and the right side of your trailer. In this case, even if you clear the car, you will be turning so tightly that the trailer may not clear the curb. I would wait for the car to move, then when that lane is clear turn the wheels a little more to the left to make a wider turn so that the trailer will clear the curb.

Generally, left hand turns are a little easier because you have more room in the intersection to swing wide. But now the obstacle is a car or truck on the left that has stopped for the light or stop sign. This is made more difficult if it's a narrow street and they've stopped too far into the intersection. In that case, if it looks as though the light's about to change, it may be best to pull up, let it change, and when they get the green they'll be out of your way. Figure 5-2 shows a left hand turn and the arrows show where you should be looking. Remember that if you get halfway through the turn and you're not going to clear the car on your left, wait for them to move. Do not back up. By this time a car may have pulled up behind you or someone could be walking behind the trailer.

Fig. 5-2. Left turn

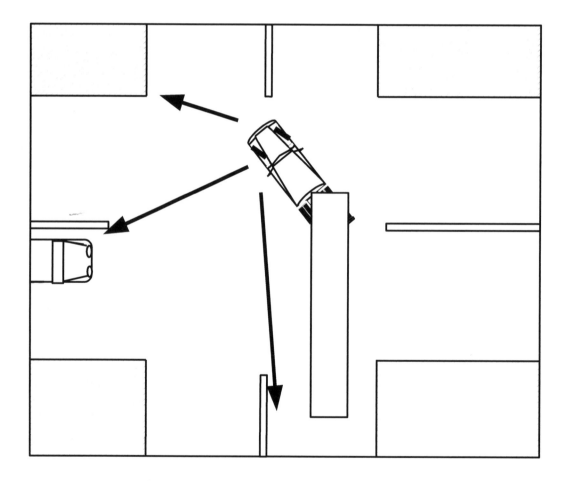

City Driving

In city traffic, while waiting at a stop sign for traffic to clear or while waiting at a red light keep your attention at the front and sides of your tractor. This is not a good time to be looking around for something in your truck. A pedestrian walking close to your truck is hard to see and they may assume that you can see them.

If you are in a large city that has highways going through it and around it, many times it's worth it to go out of your way to use the highway to get to a different part of the city if you have another delivery there. It may save you from going down a street with 20 traffic lights.

I wouldn't want to drive a truck now without a cell phone. It can be a big pain in the neck trying to find a public phone where you can park a tractor trailer. However, cell phones can be a big distraction and I'm sure you're aware by now that cell phone use is responsible for a huge number of accidents. Company policies and laws governing cell phone use can change quickly and can vary from one region to the next. You're responsible for being aware of these changes. One of my first deliveries before I carried a cell phone was in Queens, New York City. I got within a couple blocks of the warehouse but couldn't find it. Now I had to drive around looking for a phone booth, a job in itself. When I reached them on the phone one of the warehouse guys told me where they were but I still couldn't find it and had to make a second trip to the phone booth. Not a good way to start your day. A phone can be helpful even on deliveries where you know the location. Something may have changed, such as a street or an exit closed because of construction. A phone call to the customer can provide you with alternate directions. I recently had to make a delivery in Buffalo, NY. It was my first time to that location. According to the computer directions I had to make a right turn, go two blocks, then make a left onto a street running the same direction as the one I was on. However, I noticed that there was a rail line between me and the street two blocks over and I expected the worst. Sure enough, when it came time to make the right turn I saw a train overpass marked way too low for my truck so I continued straight down the street instead of turning. Looking to the right at the next intersection I saw another low overpass but this one was marked a little higher so I turned onto the street. It was still marked too low for my truck so I pulled over. You'll find that some overpasses are not marked correctly and that you will fit under them. Sometimes the roadway has been dug out to make more room but the original height sign is still on the bridge. You can try and creep under them slowly with your emergency flashers on, but if you don't fit you're going to have to back out, trying not to hit anyone behind you. You'll want to avoid this, so if the overpass is close to your customer call them on your cell phone. If it's in their neighborhood they probably know if trucks fit under the bridge. In this case, I was about three blocks away from the delivery. When I called, the owner said that if I continued on the street that I'd been on, the next side street went over the tracks instead of under them. I was able to swing around in a parking lot and get back to the first street. After the delivery I made a note about it in my directions in case I ever have to go there again, or in case I have to tell another driver how to get there.

As you get ready to leave, if it's the first time that you've delivered to that location, tell the people which way you plan on going. They may know a better way to the interstate, or whatever direction you need to go for your next delivery.

When maneuvering around city streets and parking lots, remember that whether going forward or backward you need to watch where the trailer is going as much as you need to see where you're steering the tractor. If someone has parked so close to a loading dock that it's going to make your backup next to impossible don't feel bad about asking them to move the car or truck. If you feel that you don't have the time for them to move it, think of how much time it will take to fill out an accident report.

6

Backing Basics

What does a new driver want to know about backing up a tractor trailer?

A new driver wants to know how to back up from point A (somewhere on a street or in a parking lot) to point B (an entrance, parking space, or loading dock). A new driver wants to know how to set up for the back up, when to turn the steering wheel, and how far to turn the wheel.

Before going over how to back up to a loading dock or into a parking lot I'd like to describe a few basic maneuvers. Understanding how your trailer moves will help you later on when you encounter different delivery situations. I'm hoping that talking about what I do on my job plus using diagrams helps you to visualize how you want to back up your tractor trailer.

Maneuvering a tractor trailer is not an exact science. There are too many variables involved to have an identical formula for each situation. Parking lots are different in size, you sometimes may have different size trailers, your trailer tandem wheels may be adjusted in different positions from one day to the next, and when you return to a location that you're familiar with, there will be cars or trucks parked in different spots. All of these things affect how you need to turn the steering wheel.

Why your trailer moves in the opposite direction of the steering wheel.

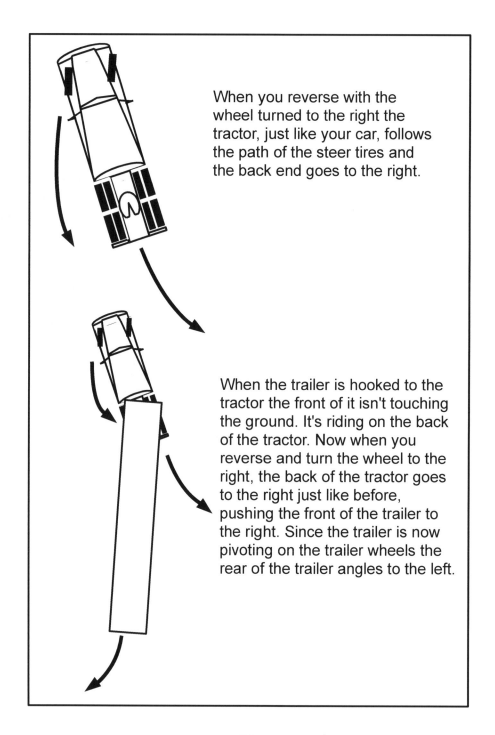

When you reverse with the wheel turned to the right the tractor, just like your car, follows the path of the steer tires and the back end goes to the right.

When the trailer is hooked to the tractor the front of it isn't touching the ground. It's riding on the back of the tractor. Now when you reverse and turn the wheel to the right, the back of the tractor goes to the right just like before, pushing the front of the trailer to the right. Since the trailer is now pivoting on the trailer wheels the rear of the trailer angles to the left.

If every parking lot and dock area were large enough to pull your tractor and trailer into a straight line in front of a loading dock or parking space you wouldn't have to worry about backing up at an angle. Of course, that doesn't happen in the real world. Getting your trailer to back up on a curved path towards a dock or parking space involves two basic maneuvers.

1. Set the angle

Setting the angle (that's what I call it, some call it jacking the trailer) means turning the steering wheel while backing in order to put the tractor and trailer at an angle with each other so that they follow a curved path while backing.

2. Following the trailer

Once you set an angle and start backing in a curved line towards a dock, entrance, or parking space, you need to get the trailer to stay on the curved path that you want it to follow. You do this by turning the steering wheel in the opposite direction of how you turned it to set the angle. If you didn't start following the trailer, the angle of the trailer would keep getting sharper until the tractor and trailer jackknifed into a tight circle. You usually start following towards the beginning of a back up.

This doesn't mean that you perform just one, then the other (unless it's a completely perfect back up). During most back ups you're adjusting the wheel as you back up, sometimes increasing the angle, sometimes increasing the amount that you're following the trailer, depending on whether the trailer is turning too sharply or not sharply enough.

Setting an Angle

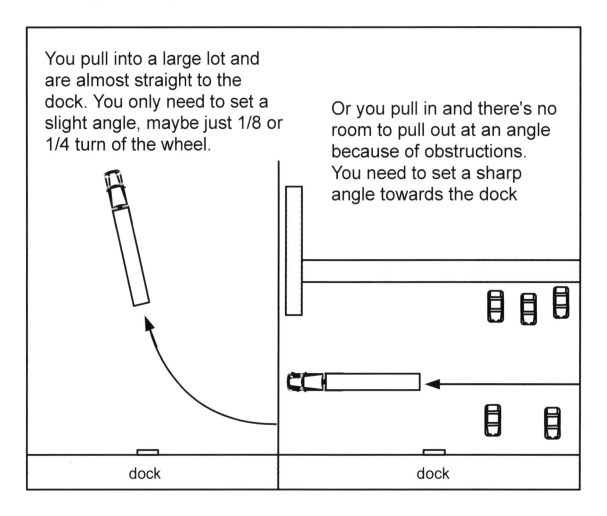

You pull into a large lot and are almost straight to the dock. You only need to set a slight angle, maybe just 1/8 or 1/4 turn of the wheel.

Or you pull in and there's no room to pull out at an angle because of obstructions. You need to set a sharp angle towards the dock

dock

dock

In both of these examples you have to get the trailer to the left so you'll be turning the steering wheel to the right to set an angle. In the example on the left it's just a slight turn to the right, and in the right example you'd probably be turning the wheel to the right as far as it would go.

Setting an angle (continued)

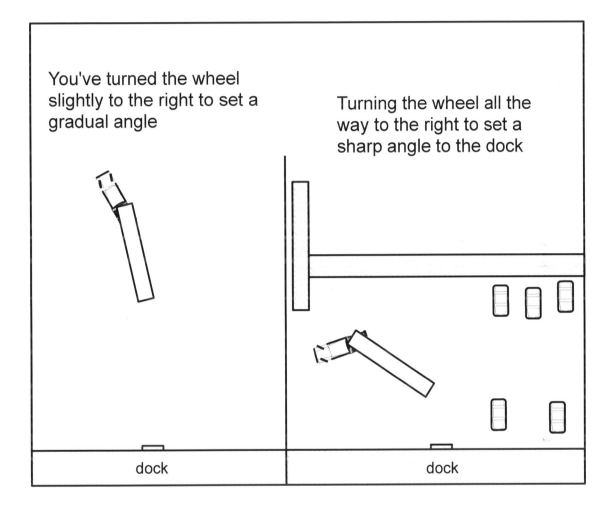

In both of these examples you've set the angle, started backing, and now it's time to follow the trailer (see next page). In the right hand example remember that when you follow the trailer, the front of the tractor swings around so you have to be careful not to hit the wall that's in front of the tractor.

Following the trailer

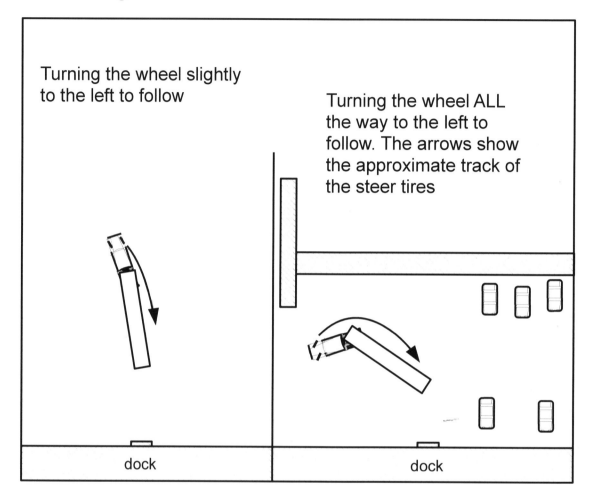

In most back ups following the trailer is similar to how you set the angle. If you set a slight, gradual angle just turn slightly to follow. If you set a sharp angle you have to turn the wheel all the way over in the opposite direction to follow.

Remember: Even when you turn the wheel just 1/8 or 1/4 turn such as the back up on the left, the longer you hold that angle while backing the sharper the angle will become between the tractor and trailer and the more you'll have to turn the wheel to follow the trailer. Even a slight angle, if held too long, will jackknife the tractor and trailer into a tight circle. In most back ups the first angle is held just long enough until you see that both units will follow the curved line that you want, then you must immediately start following.

Angle and follow

As I mentioned on the previous page, once you set the angle you want, you quickly turn the wheel in the opposite direction to follow the trailer. This is a typical 90 degree back up and you can see that most of the back up is following the trailer (wheel turned to the left). Then towards the end you turn it even harder to the left to straighten out the tractor. And of course, depending on where you start, you may be adjusting the wheel either way to follow the curve you want the tractor and trailer to follow.

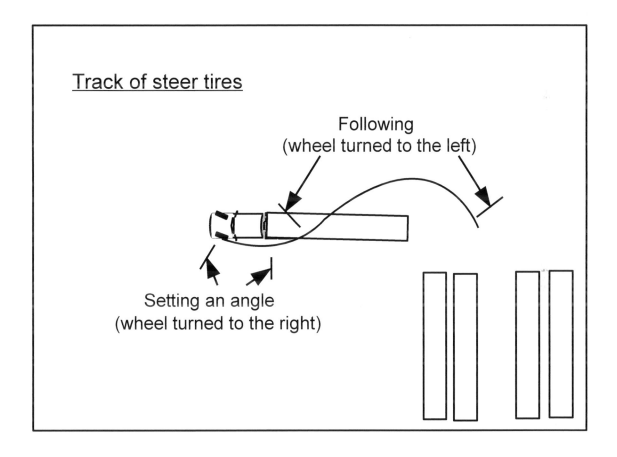

Track of steer tires

Following
(wheel turned to the left)

Setting an angle
(wheel turned to the right)

Remember: The safest back up is no back up at all. If possible pull into a space instead of backing in.

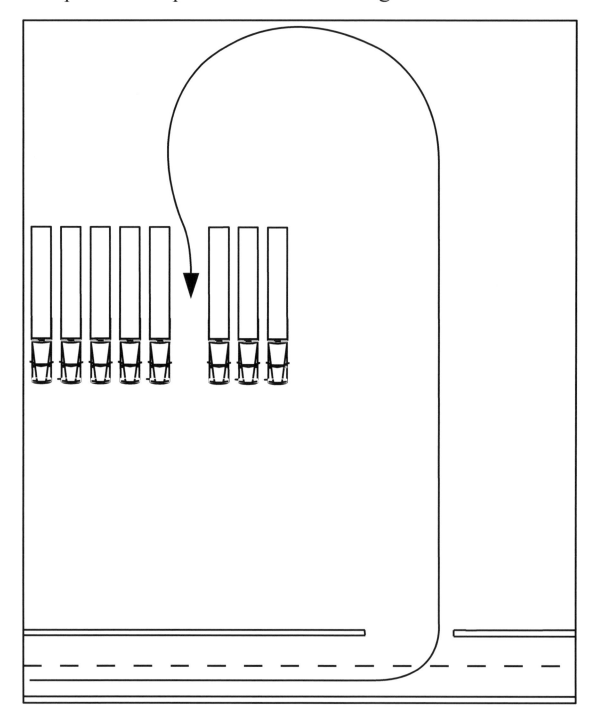

Straight back up

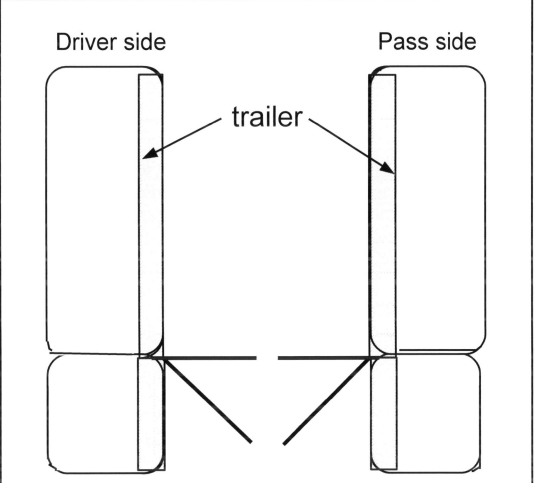

This is what I see in my mirrors as I'm driving. I have my mirrors adjusted so that the front corners of the trailer take up less than 1/4 of the mirror space. On the next page I describe a straight back up. If possible start this back up with your trailer looking like it does in this diagram. You see the front corners but you shouldn't see the sides.

Straight back up

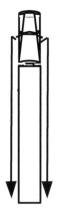

1. If possible start with the tractor and trailer in a straight line. To do this pull up or back up (4-way flashers on) until straight in the mirrors (see previous page). The arrows show your line of sight.

2. Now I back up slowly and with the back of my head up against the seat (for best line of sight) I turn my head back and forth every 2 seconds to check the left and right mirrors as I'm backing.

3. If you see both front corners of the trailer in your mirrors but not the side walls, that means you're backing straight and you don't need to turn the wheel. If one of the sides starts to appear (in this case the left) turn the top of the steering wheel 1/8 of a turn towards that side (see insert). When it starts to disappear, immediately turn the wheel back to the original position.

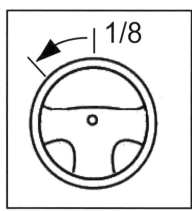

Correcting a straight back up

Although a straight back up looks easy it can take awhile for you to feel comfortable with it. First of all try to correct the trailer as soon as you see it moving to the left or right. The more it drifts before you catch it, the farther you'll have to turn the steering wheel to correct it. Then because of the delayed reaction of the steering (we'll get into that later) you end up zig zagging your way back instead of backing straight.

On the next page I show what I do when I have a straight back up that's not quite straight. I have to move the trailer over a few feet to the left or right to get it up to a dock or into a parking space.

You'll find that if you gradually angle over to the space you end up with a blind spot on the far side. So what I try to do is get the trailer over to the correct path as soon as possible, then get the tractor over to follow it on that path so that I end up in line with the target spot and I can see if there's clearance next to my trailer in both the left and right side mirrors.

Correcting a straight back up

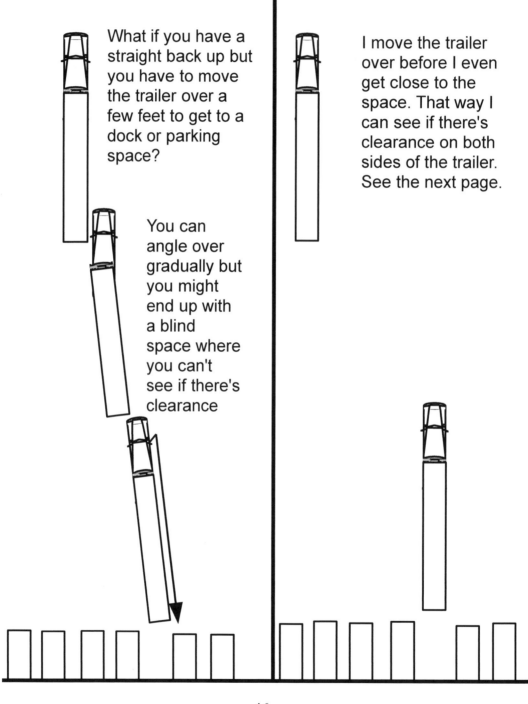

What if you have a straight back up but you have to move the trailer over a few feet to get to a dock or parking space?

You can angle over gradually but you might end up with a blind space where you can't see if there's clearance

I move the trailer over before I even get close to the space. That way I can see if there's clearance on both sides of the trailer. See the next page.

Correcting a straight back up (continued)

To shift the tractor and trailer over a few feet to the right, turn the wheel left, right , then left

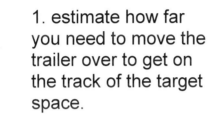

1. estimate how far you need to move the trailer over to get on the track of the target space.

2. turn the wheel to the left to make the trailer go to the right

To shift to the left, turn opposite of what's shown here. Turn right, left, then right

3. when it looks like the trailer wheels are on track turn the wheel to the right. This will swing the front of the trailer over to the right to line up with the back of the trailer

4. finally you turn back to the left to bring the front of the tractor over, then straighten out the steer tires to back into the space.

Correcting a straight back up (continued)

You've had to pull in from the left and have to back in between some trailers. There are some vehicles on the left preventing you from getting straight in front of the space. You back in but you're getting too close to the trailer on your right. What do you do?

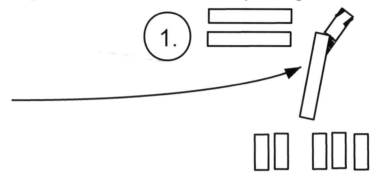

What I do is pull forward to straighten the tractor and trailer, then back up again but I wait a little longer this time before angling the tractor so that the trailer is a little more to the left of the first track.

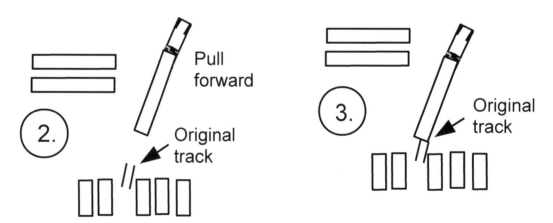

By waiting a little longer before turning the wheel to the left to angle the trailer, the back of my trailer is positioned a little more to the left than it was the first time. Now I turn the wheel to the left to start angling into the space.

Delayed reaction

Just a quick word about something that affects any backing maneuver, the delayed reaction of your steering.

You're almost up to the dock and you've got the steering wheel turned to the left so that the front of the tractor will end up straight with the trailer. If you could at this point somehow pick up the front of the tractor and move it over everything would end up straight at the dock. But because the tractor's still at an angle with the trailer, in the few feet that you'll be moving to get straight, the trailer will be moving to the left.   And look like this

You have to anticipate and start following the trailer sooner. When you're a few feet from the dock the tractor should already be straight with the trailer. When I'm off on one of my backups it's usually because the trailer is going too far to the left, like in this diagram, and it means that I didn't start following the trailer soon enough. More about this later.

Parallel parking

1. To parallel park to a curb on your passenger side turn the steering wheel 1/4 turn to the left to angle the trailer towards the curb. (To park to a curb on your left perform all of these steps in the opposite direction.)

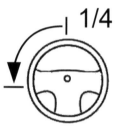

2. In the right side mirror I watch the right side trailer tires and when they are about 1 foot from the curb I stop the truck, turn the wheel 2 full turns to the right, and then continue backing. This brings the front of the trailer to the right to line up with the curb. Note: WHEN you turn the wheel depends on how far away you are from the curb. If you're far away you don't want to hold that first angle so long that you jack knife and lose sight of the curb. You may have to turn the wheel a little to the right BEFORE you get close to the curb so that you can still see both the trailer tires and the curb in your mirror while backing.

Parallel parking (continued)

3. When the trailer is almost parallel to the curb I turn the wheel 2 full turns to the left to bring the front of the tractor around to the right so it's parallel to the curb.

Note: I said turn the wheel to the left when ALMOST parallel to the curb. There's a delay in the trailer reaction after you turn the wheel. You should cut the wheel to the left a little before the trailer is parallel because it will continue moving slightly to the right as you bring the front of the tractor over to the right.

4. Now you should be parallel to the curb. The only thing left to do is straighten your wheels and possibly pull ahead a little to finish straightening the tractor and trailer. So there are basically 3 turns of the steering wheel, starting opposite of whichever side you're backing. To park to a curb on your right, turn left, right, then left.

Here's two things I think about when backing. This first one is about backing up to a dock or parking space.

Backing track

You'll find that it's easier to pull out of a parking space than it is to back into a space. So it follows that the best way to back in to a space is to get your trailer tires to follow the same track that they make when leaving a parking space.

Since this book is roughly organized in chronological order (a typical work day from start to finish) I saved the last chapter to describe backing into a space along a row of trucks such as you might find at a truck stop at the end of the day.

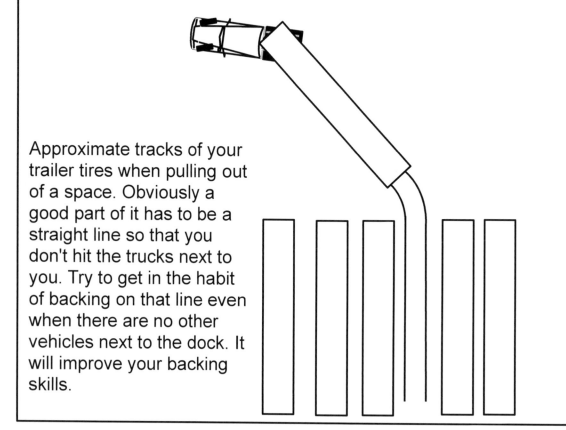

Approximate tracks of your trailer tires when pulling out of a space. Obviously a good part of it has to be a straight line so that you don't hit the trucks next to you. Try to get in the habit of backing on that line even when there are no other vehicles next to the dock. It will improve your backing skills.

Backing track (continued)

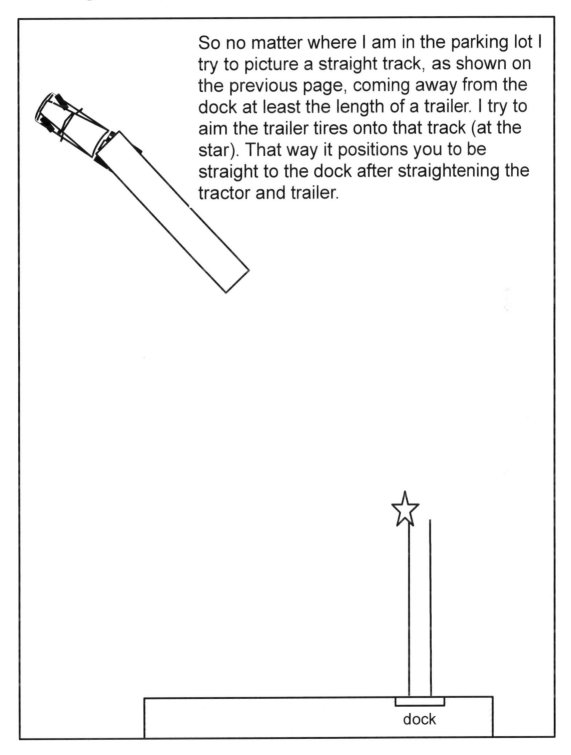

So no matter where I am in the parking lot I try to picture a straight track, as shown on the previous page, coming away from the dock at least the length of a trailer. I try to aim the trailer tires onto that track (at the star). That way it positions you to be straight to the dock after straightening the tractor and trailer.

dock

Backing track (continued)

This is another look at what I'm talking about. Instead of just angling towards the dock from wherever I am in the lot (dotted lines) I try to place the trailer tires on a straight line from the dock, a trailer length away from the dock if possible (solid lines). Then I finish angling in to straighten up to the dock.

Of course it's possible to come in at a sharp angle like the dotted lines and then turn your wheel hard to straighten the trailer but chances are your tractor won't be straight. There may be no vehicles next to you when you back in but if there are open docks next to you another driver wouldn't be able to back up to the dock with your tractor at an angle. And if a driver tried to back in next to you there would be more chance of your tractor getting hit if it was on an angle.

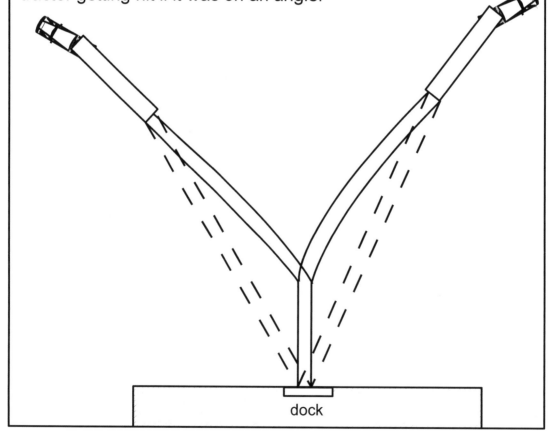

dock

The other basic rule I try to follow is to get the back of my trailer close to where it has to go.

If you pulled up and had to back into this entrance you'd run out of room to swing the tractor around if you weren't over to the left.

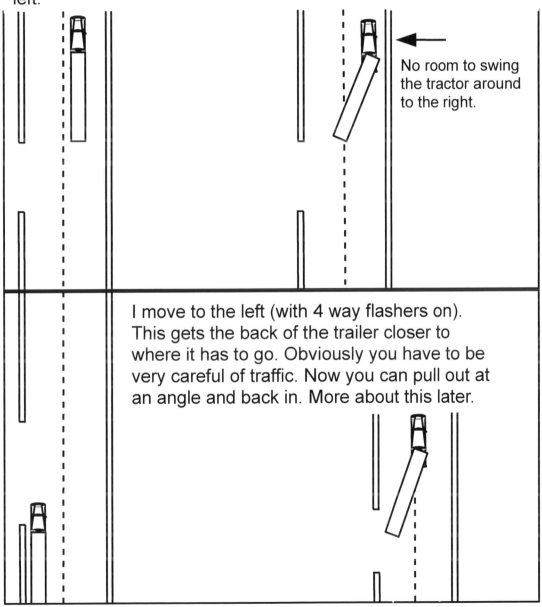

No room to swing the tractor around to the right.

I move to the left (with 4 way flashers on). This gets the back of the trailer closer to where it has to go. Obviously you have to be very careful of traffic. Now you can pull out at an angle and back in. More about this later.

There are different ways that drivers think about how to turn the steering wheel when backing up. They include:

1. turning the wheel in the opposite direction that you want the trailer to go.
2. turn the top of the wheel towards any obstacle that you want to avoid.
3. grab the bottom of the wheel and turn it in the same direction that you want the trailer to go.

You can experiment with these to see what works best for you. After you've been driving for awhile you won't have to think about it as much. In this book when I describe turning the wheel left or right I mean the top of the wheel. If I had to describe what I'm thinking when I back up I'd have to say that when I'm backing at an angle I picture a curved line, al-most part of a circle, that I want the tractor and trailer wheels to follow. When I want to make that curve wider, so that the trailer goes more towards the far side, I turn the steering wheel towards the center of the circle. If I want to turn sharper I turn away from the circle. See the diagram below. I'm just offering it to show how I think of it but as I said, see what works best for you.

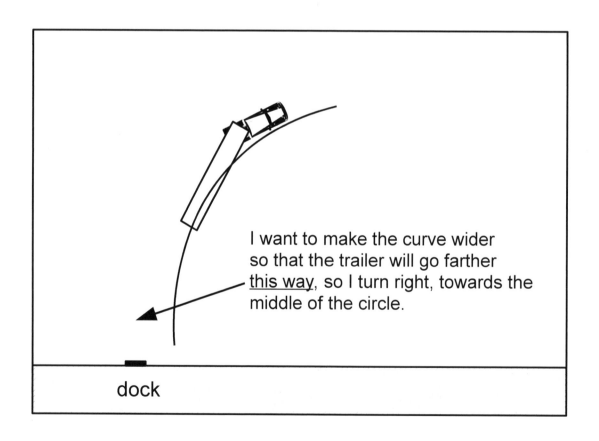

I want to make the curve wider so that the trailer will go farther this way, so I turn right, towards the middle of the circle.

dock

7

Back up to the Dock

Although the title of this chapter is Back Up To The Dock, there's a good chance that you won't always be backing up to a dock. A customer may have you back up between some parked cars to a spot in the middle of a parking lot where someone on a fork truck lifts something off of the back of your trailer. Or they may have you back up to an overhead door. That's not to say you're necessarily going to fit through the door. Anytime that you're not backing up to a loading dock you need to use extra care when backing up close to a building. There are no rubber bumpers like you find on a dock to protect the building. If you hit the wall or the top edge of an overhead door opening, you're going to damage it. From where you're sitting it's hard to see the back of your trailer. Before you get too close this is a good time for G.O.A.L., the acronym often used in safety meetings which stands for Get Out And Look. This applies to any difficult backup, especially blind side backups. It's better to get out of your truck to check two or three times, if necessary, rather than having to call your company to tell them that you've damaged a building, a parked car, or a truck.

Speaking of damaging anything, if it seems unfair that certain companies require one or two years experience before hiring you, it's because they don't want their insurance costs rising because of accidents. They know that a new driver is more likely to put scrapes and dents in trucks, cars, and buildings. They know that the more experienced you are, the more you realize just how careful you have to be to avoid these things. So it follows that the more careful you are, the quicker that you'll get to the point where you have more of a choice in what kind of job you can get and what kind of company will hire you. It's also important to try to keep any traffic tickets off of your record whether you're driving a truck or your car. One of the first things a company will do when you apply for a job is to run your license number through the computer. The cleaner your record is, the more likely you'll hear back from them.

If you have a delivery appointment make sure that you leave early enough to get there on time. The customer may have scheduled people to be there for unloading your truck. They may also have another truck scheduled to unload after your truck. If you're late they may start the other truck first, making your day a lot longer. When you're working on your directions to get to a delivery, estimate the amount of time to get there. Figure in some extra time for rush hour traffic if your delivery is in a city. If you use a website to estimate your driving time you should always add a little extra time, either because of road construction in the summer, bad weather in the winter, or climbing hills if your truck is heavy. If you know that you're going to be late it's a good idea to call ahead. That helps the customer rearrange their schedule. Always try to be on time but never at the expense of safety.

As you approach your delivery reduce your distractions. Turn down the radio, turn off the CB, and don't take any phone calls. You may have to pull up to the curb to wait for a break in traffic or to open your trailer doors if you'll be backing up close to other trailers. Turn on your emergency flashers and be careful opening your doors in traffic. Always get in the habit of fastening your swing doors when they're open. You don't want a gust of wind taking out someone's windshield with your door. When I first started driving I had to make a delivery with a straight truck that had swing doors. I forgot to fasten the passenger side door when I opened it. Then I was directed to back up further, to a spot that put me next to a building. When I was done I couldn't close the door without moving the truck, so I thought that I'd close them after pulling out into the street. I pulled out into the street and when I looked at my right side mirror I saw the door swing around. It just missed hitting the side mirror on a parked car. Of course if you have a roll-up door make a mental note to close it immediately after each delivery. After you're back in the cab there's no way to see if your door is closed by looking in the mirror.

If you are going to a location for the first time, don't automatically pull into their lot. If it's a small parking lot you may have to back in from the street to get up to a loading dock. Make a visual note of anything in the area where you have to back in such as overhangs, low wires, or cars or trucks parked nearby. This is a good time to talk out loud to yourself (called commentary driving). Before you pull out into the yard or the street to begin your backup and lose sight of the dock area, you can say something like "There's a red car on the left, white truck on the right". Now, when you've pulled up to start your backup, you know what to look for in your mirrors. Before angling out into the street or the yard to start your backup, make one last check in your mirrors for traffic, or pedestrians that may be crossing behind you.

Back up to the Dock

The biggest piece of advice that I can give for backing up is to take your time. Don't let anyone rush you. That includes traffic. You have a much greater chance of correcting the angle of the trailer if you're backing up slowly.

Remember this: ALMOST ANY PROBLEM INVOLVED WITH BACKING CAN BE SOLVED BY GOING SLOWLY.

One of my customers is at an area where you have to back across three lanes of traffic, just beyond a blind curve. One of the guys in the shop comes out and stops the traffic. With that many people waiting on you the tendency is to rush your way through it. But it's actually quicker to take your time to get it right the first time instead of hurrying, getting into the wrong angle, and having to pull up and start over again. There will be times, such as making a turn into a narrow street, that you can't avoid getting people annoyed with you by taking up extra space. But if you don't give yourself enough room and get stuck halfway through a turn, no one will be able to move.

If you've spent the night at a warehouse parking lot and someone wakes you up by knocking on your door telling you to back up to the dock, give yourself a couple minutes to wake up. This is a good time to get out of the truck, get some fresh air, and take a quick look behind the trailer to refresh your memory of any obstacles near the dock. It also gives you a chance to see if anyone has parked near your truck since you pulled in the night before.

Backing in from the street

I'm sure that you know by now that it's preferable to approach your delivery so that the dock will be on your left side. It's much easier to see out of your driver side mirror and window than it is to see out of the right side. If you go to a location on a regular basis, you may find that it's worth it to go out of your way a little bit in order to approach from that direction. But you'll also find that sometimes a blind side backup can't be avoided, such as when a customer is on a one way street.

Scan this area when pulling up. Make sure the area is wide enough for your trailer and make note of vehicles, overhangs, low hanging wires, and other obstructions.

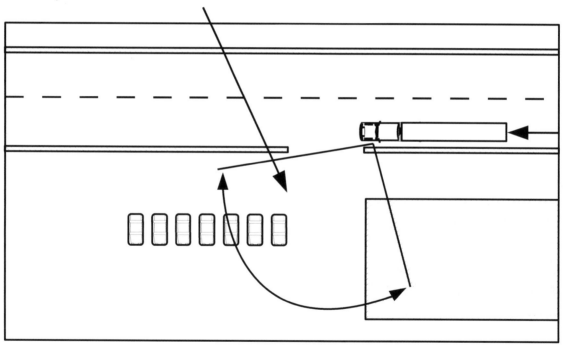

Backing in from the street (continued)

One advantage of calling ahead to a location that you've never been to before is that they can tell you if you have to back in from the street or whether you can pull in, then back up to a dock. If I know that I have to back in from the street and I'm able to have the entrance on my left, the first thing I do is check for traffic in front of me and behind me. If it's all clear I turn on my emergency flashers and pull over to the left before getting even with the entrance so that the rear of the trailer will be over on the left side of the street. You always want to get the rear of the trailer close to the entrance. If you started your backup from the right side of the street your tractor would be up against the right curb before you even got halfway through your backup. Driving by the entrance I continue until the rear of the trailer is almost even with the entrance and then, after checking my right mirror once more for traffic, I pull out to the right so the trailer is close to a 45 degree angle across the street with the rear of the trailer pointed towards the entrance. Before coming to a stop I angle the tractor slightly to the left. This helps me to see the rear of the trailer and it sets up the tractor and trailer for a good angle to back in to the entrance. Sometimes, because of traffic, or if you have to open your doors first, you won't be able to do this in one motion. In that case, turn on your left signal, pull over to the left curb before you get to the entrance, then turn on your emergency flashers. When traffic clears, pull out to your 45 degree angle.

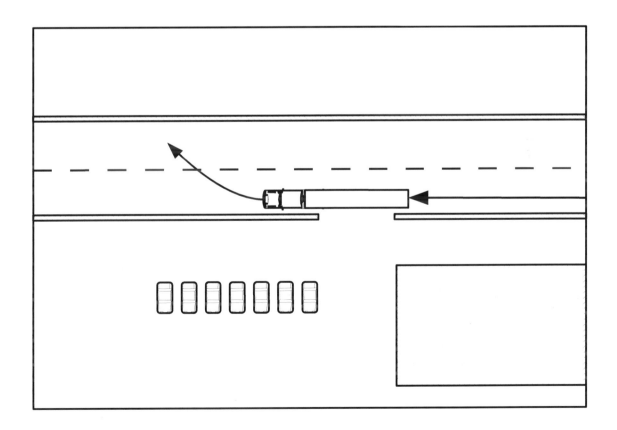

Backing in from the street (continued)

There will be many situations where you won't have enough room to even get close to a 45 degree angle. The important thing is to get the rear of the trailer over to the left and to get far enough past the entrance so that you can see both the left rear of your trailer and the edge of the entrance in your mirror at the same time. Now that you can see both the trailer and the entrance, start backing up slowly so you can keep them both in your mirror and that you keep the trailer pointed so it will just clear that side of the entrance as you back up. You'll be moving your eyes back and forth, from your left mirror to check on the trailer, to the right side of your tractor to make sure that you don't hit anything as you start to swing your tractor to the right to follow your trailer. As the trailer starts into the entrance there's going to be room for cars to get around the right front of your tractor. You'll be thinking that no one in their right mind will try and get around the front of your tractor when they see that you have to swing it to the right to follow the trailer. But they WILL drive through the opening so you have to go slowly at this point, check your right mirror, and be ready to stop if someone comes through before you swing the tractor to the right.

Your setup is complete. The steer tires are back straight in the original position and the black arrow shows your line of sight (being able to see the rear of the trailer and the curb).

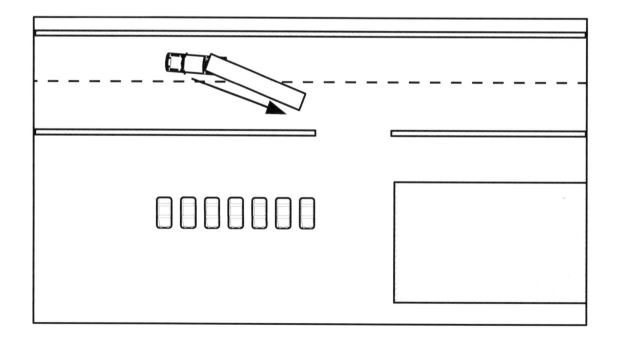

Backing in from the street (continued)

After you swing your tractor to follow the trailer you should be lined up straight in order to back into the entrance. If not, check for traffic, then pull ahead to adjust the angle to whichever side you need in order to be centered. Now you check both mirrors to make sure that you're clear on both sides as you back in through the entrance. Use this same procedure to do a see side backup into a loading dock lane, or a parking space. Get the rear of the trailer over to the left, pull past the dock lane or parking space, then angle out until you can see both the lane and your trailer in the mirror. There's a more detailed explanation in the last chapter about backing into a tight parking space. A dock lane or parking space is going to be tighter than a street entrance so take your time. If you're getting too close to a trailer or truck pull ahead a little ways so that you can get a straighter angle and repeat this, if necessary, until you can see clearance in both of your mirrors.

In some situations there may be cars parked on the opposite side of the street, reducing the amount of room that you'll need to swing the tractor around to follow the trailer into the entrance . You can solve this by pulling a little further down the street before your backup, and then backing in at a more gradual angle. If there are no obstructions inside the entrance this allows you to get the rear of the trailer part of the way into the entrance before you have to start swinging the tractor around to follow it. You may have to do a couple pull ups to get straight, but it may be the only way to get in and still be able to clear the parked cars. You can also try adjusting the trailer tandems forward.

You'll find that some docks are so close to the street that your tractor will be sticking out into a traffic lane after you're up to the dock. Ask if they have any yellow safety cones that you can put on both sides of the front of your tractor. I've had police tell me that they would give me a ticket unless I put out some safety cones. The company that you're delivering to has probably had to deal with this before so the chances are good that they keep safety cones available for you to use. At a location where the street is so narrow that you'll be blocking a lane of traffic it helps if you can angle the tractor to leave room on the street. This is a little tricky and takes some practice. As you get close to the dock while backing, start following your trailer a little sooner so that it looks as though you'll be a little further over on the far side of the dock. At the last minute crank the wheel over hard so that the nose of the tractor will be out of the traffic lane as much as possible. The trick is not to cut the wheel hard too soon. Wait until you're only a foot or two from the dock because when you start a sharp angle like that the trailer stops going backwards and just starts to pivot, and it won't end up straight to the dock .

Malls

If you have to deliver to a store in a mall you'll probably find out that they're not very truck friendly. The first challenge is just getting into the mall. At one location I have to approach with the mall on my right. This makes for a tighter turn than if you were turning from the far side of the street. Not only is the entrance narrow but they often make it worse by putting a median in the middle of the entrance to separate the incoming and outgoing traffic. I move over to the second lane from the curb (being very careful about watching any traffic that might come up from behind on my right). Even after moving over to that lane the trailer tires go over the curb on the corner of the entrance when I pull in. Luckily it's a low curb with no light poles or signs near it.

Things to remember about mall deliveries

1. It doesn't hurt to call ahead. They might be able to tell you the best entrance to use. One place directed me to a separate truck entrance nowhere near the main entrance.
2. As I said above, be prepared to make a VERY wide swing to get into the mall. Most deliveries are in the back of the mall. As soon as you enter the mall you may see a sign pointing you in the direction for truck traffic. If not, most truck lanes are either left or right as soon as you enter the mall, around the outside edges of the main parking lot to take you behind the mall.
3. Make it easy on yourself when exiting the mall. If it's a very large mall with numerous exits, some with stop signs, some with traffic lights, pick one with a light. Better to wait a couple minutes for a light to change than waiting for traffic to clear on a busy four lane road.

Back up to the Dock

Here's a typical setup many drivers use for backing into a parking space or up to a dock. Unlike the previous examples, this is for a parking lot where you have more room than you would have in a street. See Chapter 11 for tips on backing into tight spaces at small truck stops. This diagram uses a row of trailers such as you'd find at a warehouse. Do this all in one motion starting about 8 to 10 feet away from the row of trailers. When your tractor drive wheels reach the closest edge of the space cut the wheel hard to the right. The turning radius of your tractor and the length of your trailer could affect when to make this first turn, so experiment with it. You might be making this turn before your drive wheels reach the space, or after they reach the space. When you reach the position in fig. 2 (when your tractor is facing the same direction as the parked trailers), cut your wheel hard to the left and stop when you are at a right angle to the trailers (fig 3). You should now be set up for backing into the space.

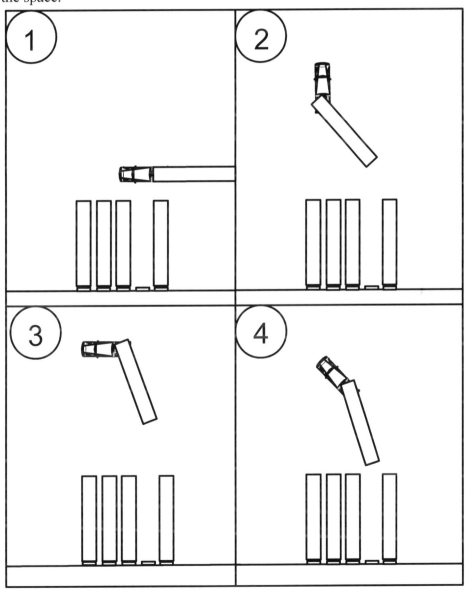

Blind Side Backing

You're going to use the same procedures for blind side backing, except that it's much harder to see what's going on because you're sitting on the opposite side of the entrance or dock space. To blind side into a street entrance on the right side of the street, pull up to the right side curb before the entrance and turn on your emergency flashers. When traffic clears use the same procedure I described on pg. 60 and angle out into the street. Now you'll be looking to keep the right rear of your trailer and the left side of the entrance in the right side mirror. If you have a motorized adjustable mirror now is the time to use it because as you angle the tractor around you'll quickly lose sight of the right rear of your trailer unless you have a day cab with a window in the back wall. Using the toggle switch for the mirror, adjust the mirror out to keep the back of the trailer in sight as you back into the entrance. You may still have to get out of the tractor or stop and lean over the passenger seat to see if you're clearing the entrance. Use the same procedure for blind side backing into a dock lane and pulling forward more than once, if necessary, to get straight into the dock lane. The angles will be the same as in the previous diagrams only now you'll be coming in from the other direction.

Straight Back Up

If you're backing up to a dock in a large parking lot with no obstructions opposite the dock, the easiest procedure is a straight backup. I use the same approach as shown in steps 1 and 2 on pg. 65 except I turn out a little sooner. If there is a truck in the space just before the empty space, I continue until I can see the entire empty space out of my driver side window, then I turn hard to the right. I hold the angle for a few seconds, then straighten out so that my tractor and trailer are parallel with the row of trucks. Start watching your mirrors before you finish straightening out and you'll get an idea of how well you're lining up to the space. You want to get the rear of the trailer pointed towards the space. Then back up slowly, making small adjustments with the steering wheel to keep the trailer in line with the space.

Remember that the trailer will react differently depending on the length of the trailer and the position of the tandems (the axle assembly of the trailer). The longer the trailer, the slower it reacts to any turn of your steering wheel. A short pup trailer can be more difficult to back up than a long trailer because just a slight turn of the wheel can make the trailer turn too far in the opposite direction. There's a good chance that you'll be pulling a trailer with adjustable tandems. On such a trailer your rear trailer axles can be slid forward or backward. The purpose of this is to evenly distribute the weight of your entire vehicle on the road surface. Each state has laws concerning the weight of the load on different axles. Basically, the more that you move the trailer axle forward, getting them under the load, the more weight you take off of the tractor axles. The position of your trailer axles also affects how your trailer turns. Since the actual pivoting of your trailer is done on the wheels, the further ahead that they are adjusted the quicker the trailer will react, just as though you had a smaller trailer. Because it reacts quicker getting around obstacles, the general rule is that the more they are adjusted forward, the easier it is to get around tight turns such as you'll find in city traffic or small parking lots. The only problem is that you haven't reduced the actual length of your trailer. You have to account for the overhang, the section of your trailer behind the axles. When you have the tandems adjusted forward, you can get around obstacles easier but that overhang is going to swing out wider than it would if the axles were adjusted all the way to the back. This means, for example, that if you are pulling out of a tight parking space with vehicles on both sides, you need to pull straight ahead as far as possible in order to clear those vehicles before turning or the vehicle on the opposite side could get hit by the overhang as it swings around. That also means that when the tandems are adjusted forward you can't back into the space at too much of an angle or you'll hit the vehicle on the opposite side with the overhang. You need to get the trailer pointed straighter into the space sooner than you would have to if the tandems had been adjusted towards the rear of the trailer.

To adjust the tandems on your trailer you should be parked on a level surface, preferably one that is paved, so that the trailer tires don't slide. Set your parking brakes and walk back to release the locking pins on your trailer tandems. On the older trailers this is done by pulling a release handle. Newer trailers are equipped with locks that are released with an air pressure button near the tandem frame. Get back into the tractor and leaving the red trailer brake button out (keeping the brakes applied on the trailer), push in the yellow parking button releasing the tractor brakes. Now you can slide the trailer forward or backwards on the tandem frame to whatever position you need. (If the pins didn't retract when you pulled the handle or pushed the air release button, slightly pull or push against the trailer once to release the pins then move the trailer forward or backward as described above). When you stop and set your parking brake chances are that the pins are not lined up with the locking holes. Not to worry. Get out and release the locking handle or reset the air lock, whichever applies to your trailer. If the pins are not exactly lined up to the holes they are now pushing up against the frame and will pop through and lock as soon as you move the trailer forward or backward. So now you get back in the tractor and once again leaving the trailer brakes set, release the tractor brakes. Slowly back up or go forward until you feel the tractor pulling against the trailer. This means that the pins have popped back into the locking holes and are preventing you from moving. Set your parking brake and go back to check that the pins have extended into the locking holes. My company uses newer trailers with air activated locking pins. I've noticed that when resetting them it's not enough to just push the button like it says on the sticker next to the button. You have to push and hold the button in until you hear the air pressure stop.

Another look at how the position of the tandems affect the trailer

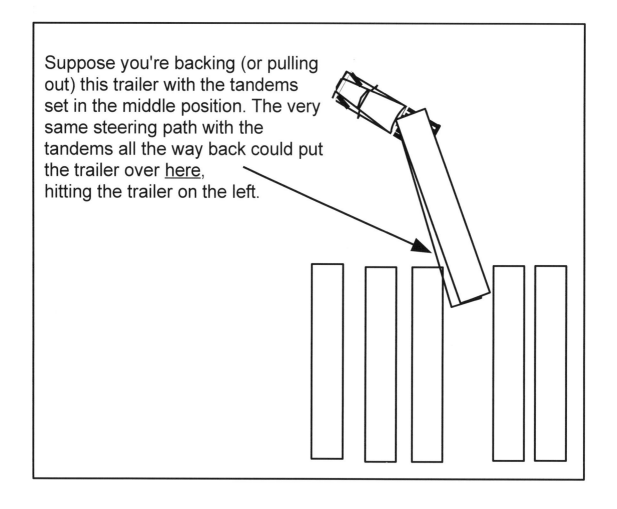

Suppose you're backing (or pulling out) this trailer with the tandems set in the middle position. The very same steering path with the tandems all the way back could put the trailer over <u>here</u>,
hitting the trailer on the left.

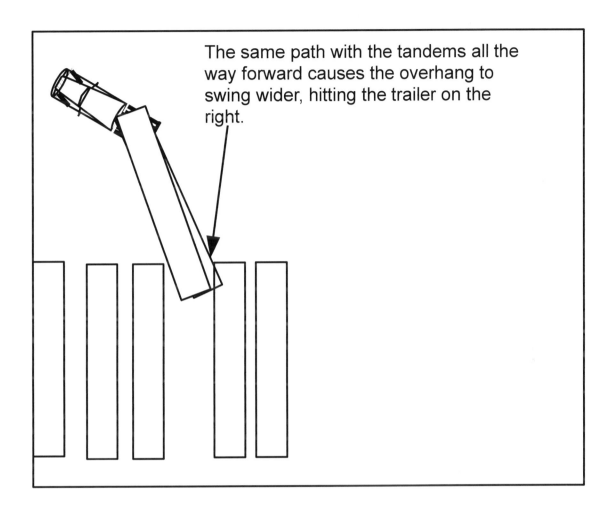

The same path with the tandems all the way forward causes the overhang to swing wider, hitting the trailer on the right.

Another way to look at how your tandems affect your back up is to see the difference between a short trailer and a long trailer. Having your tandems all the way forward is similar to how a short trailer reacts. In this diagram the steering track and position of the tractor on the right has been reproduced exactly as the one on the left. They each push the front of the trailers the same distance to the side as they back up. But the trailer on the right (roughly drawn equivalent to a 28 foot pup trailer) is at a sharper angle than the 53 foot trailer because the length from its wheels to where it pivots on the tractors fifth wheel is shorter.

When you set your angle with the tandems forward don't turn the steering wheel as far as you would for a trailer with the tandems all the way back.

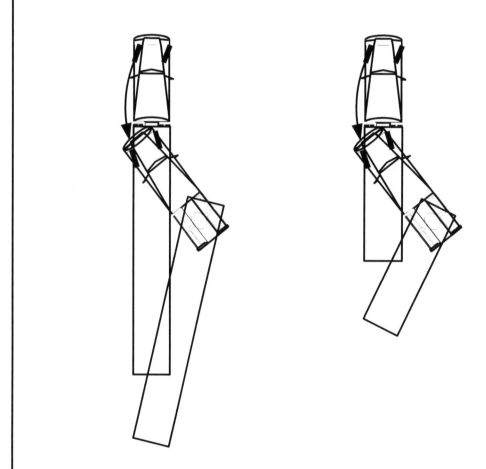

On this delivery I was accustomed to using a trailer with the tandems in the middle position or set forward. I pull over to the right and when traffic clears I pull forward and when the middle of the trailer goes by the center of the entrance I angle out across the street to set up for my back up.

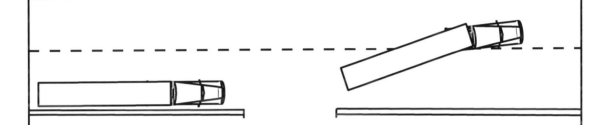

Usually I would end up in the middle of the driveway. But the first time I went there with the tandems all the way back I found that when I did my usual set up, the back of the trailer ended up way over on the far side of the entrance as shown in the lower diagram. This is what happens when the length of your rig is increased (going from a short trailer to a long trailer) or your wheel base is increased (tandems slid to the back). The curve of your back up becomes wider and you need to compensate for it. On the next page I'll show a couple suggestions of what you can do.

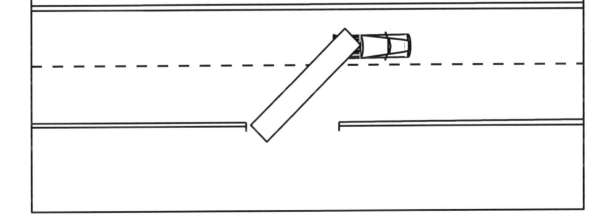

To make the back up on the previous page a little easier when the tandems are all the way back, I go a little further along the curb before pulling out to set up. I wait until the rear of the trailer is almost at the center of the entrance before pulling out. Then I angle out gradually until I can see both the right rear corner of the trailer and the edge of the entrance curb in my right mirror.

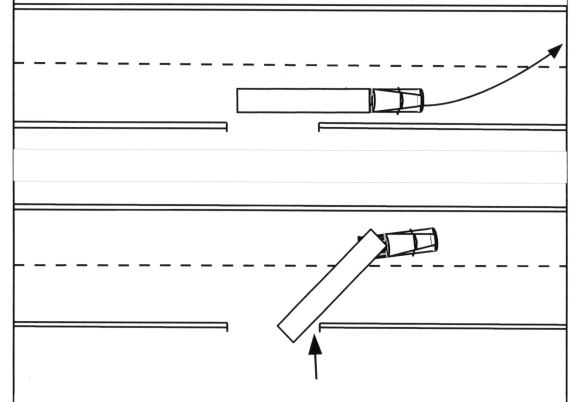

Watch your trailer tires and keep them as close as possible to this side of the entrance

This gets some of your trailer into the entrance so that you have more room on the opposite side of the street to swing the front of the tractor around. If you still don't have enough room you can try pulling back up to the curb and moving your tandems forward.

Back up to the Dock

This diagram shows a type of accident that is fairly common for truck stops. Don't let it happen to you. You're coming around a row of trucks and see a lot of open space in front of you and for a moment you forget that your trailer isn't in that open space yet. Also, you may be distracted by looking for a place to park and may be tired after a long day of work. Don't forget to be watching your trailer in the mirror as you go around other vehicles in a parking lot. This is another example of how your tandems affect the track of your trailer. The further back that your tandems are set, the more likely that something like this happens because the off track of your trailer is wider when the tandems are set back.

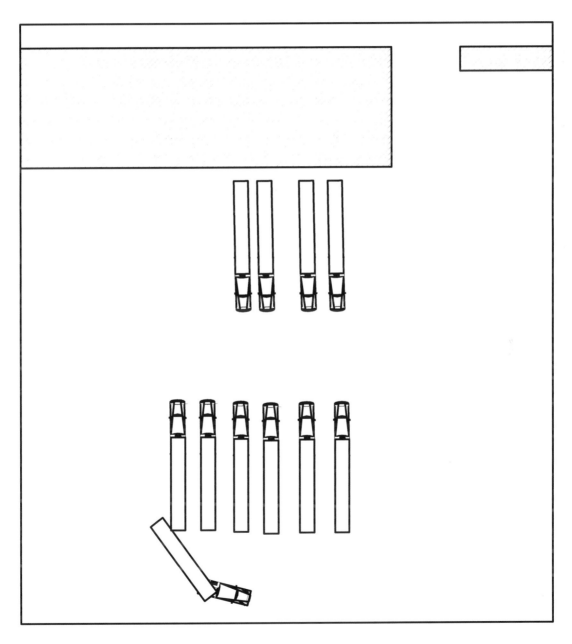

Backing up to a dock in the winter can make a tough job even harder. You've got to deal with parking lots that are smaller because the piles of snow force the cars to park further in from the edges of the lot. And the areas around the entrances where you need to cut close to the curb are now filled in with snow. You may have to pull your trailer wheels through the edge of a snow bank to get into the lot. Once you are up to the dock your troubles may not be over.

Pulling away from the dock when you're on ice and snow can be worse than getting up to the dock, especially if you're on a ramp that inclines down towards the building. If you've unloaded your total load at that location, your trailer is now lighter over the tractor drive wheels, giving you even less traction. The only way out may be to shovel and spread salt under your tires, or calling a tow truck in an extreme situation. It's possible to get stuck at a dock even when you are sitting on an almost level area. If there is ice under the snow and you back up to the dock when your tires are still warm from going down the road, they'll melt into the ice just enough to form a little depression that's almost impossible to pull out of without melting the ice in front of your tires with salt. If you have time, let you truck sit for a few minutes in the parking lot before backing up to the dock so that your tires have time to cool down.

Back up to the Dock

8

Attitude

I think the most important part of your attitude while driving a tractor trailer is to realize that the rest of the world isn't going to move out of your way just because you are behind schedule. When you're in too much of a hurry you're going to get into trouble. This holds true whether you are on a highway, in city traffic, or backing up to a dock. Your truck isn't going to react like your car so you have to take your time.

When you have a long distance, over the road job, the tendency of most drivers, myself included, is to think about getting the trip over with so that you can get home. You're kind of living in the future, in anticipation of being home for a couple days at the end of the week, or two weeks, or a month, depending on your schedule. This is only natural, but it can set you up for a higher stress level when things don't go as planned. I worked with a driver once who never seemed to be upset about any delay time because he was completely happy to be out there on the road. His time at work didn't seem any less important to him than his time at home. I'm not saying to forget about getting your job done, but it's important to concentrate on what you're doing when you're doing it. For most of us, unless you are a lottery winner, a great part of our lives is spent at work. If you're constantly thinking about getting it over with, you might as well be thinking about getting most of your life over with. Think about what you are doing when you are doing it and you might even get some enjoyment out of it.

Part of your job is to keep your cool. This job is not like punching in at a time clock and working an eight hour shift. While there are some driving jobs with set hours, many tractor trailer jobs are different from one day to the next. You may work for 5 hours one day, and 14 the next. At the beginning of your day, you can figure out a rough idea of where you will be during the day. That's helpful if you have to call ahead to give a customer your approximate arrival time. But if you try to hold yourself to a schedule every day, you can wear yourself out from stress. There are many things on this job that can cause delays, such as bad weather, equipment breakdowns, accidents, traffic, and warehouse crews that are too busy to unload you as quickly as you thought they would. You'll learn that being patient is the first step to becoming a safe truck driver. For example, when pulling out onto a two lane road, unlike driving a car, you have to wait for a break in traffic coming from both directions because of how far you have to pull out in order to clear the curb with your trailer tires. You also have to wait for longer breaks in traffic than you would with a car, because of the longer time it takes to accelerate after making your turn. As mentioned in the highway driving chapter, you need to be patient when passing another vehicle. You'll develop a sense of how long it's going to take to get around someone, depending on their speed in relation to yours and the road conditions. If you see traffic coming up fast behind you, be patient and let them go by first.

You know the consequences of tailgating at high speeds, so if someone passes you and stays on your front bumper or if you come up to a slow vehicle and can't immediately pass them, back off a little bit. Don't let them control the situation.

An important part of good attitude is good communication between you and your company. If a delivery is short on the number of pieces of freight, or if anything is damaged let your company know about it. Let them know if something doesn't get delivered because of bad weather or a customer refusal. It helps them to make alternate plans as soon as possible. Be honest about reporting delay time. Many trucks now have GPS systems and your company can see where, and for how long you've been stopped. If anything about a delivery doesn't go as planned put it in writing on your time sheet if you use one, and if anyone refuses a delivery get their name. If you're dropping a trailer at a location and picking up another trailer put it in writing on your time sheet, even if you're entering it into a computer. It's just a way to make sure that you are getting paid for your work and it helps the company keep track of their equipment.

A good attitude with your customer can go a long way in making your work day easier. Good communication with them is just as important as good communication with your company. As stated earlier you'll find that it's helpful to certain customers, as well as yourself, to notify them of any delay time. I've also found that it helps to put yourself in the shoes of the dockworkers. They've got a tough job, and if you were in their place you wouldn't be inclined to cooperate with some driver walking in the door demanding to be unloaded. If I show up at a place 15 minutes before their lunch break with a trailer that's going to take an hour to unload, I don't expect them to take a late lunch. However, if you develop a good relationship with dock workers you may find that they'll often take a late lunch in order to get you unloaded and on your way.

Attitude

A chapter about attitude should include at least one paragraph about the importance of developing good judgment. When a situation arises, judgment is that little voice in your head that asks "How important is this?" and "What should I do about it?". If you make a good decision then that's good judgment. Take it from someone who's made more than his fair share of poor decisions. It's a big part of your job. Whenever I've messed up on this job I tried to figure out what I did wrong. Sometimes it was lack of preparation such as not getting detailed directions. Sometimes I made mistakes because I was impatient and running late for an appointment. Whatever the reason was, it boiled down to the fact that I hadn't used good judgment. To me, good judgment means weighing all of your options, and then choosing the best one in any given situation. By that definition you first have to be aware of all the options available. Your judgment can be hampered by not realizing how many choices you have. For instance, let's say that you're traveling on a highway in the right hand lane and see an emergency vehicle with another vehicle on the right hand shoulder close to your lane of travel. There are cars on your left side, preventing you from moving over into the passing lane. You may think that you'll just have to barrel on through and hope that no one steps in front of your truck. You have another option. You can slow down and turn on your left turn signal light. By slowing down and letting some of the cars go by, an opening in traffic might come up allowing you to move over, and by signaling you just may alert someone courteous enough to slow down and let you move over. There are many situations that allow more than one course of action, or inaction. You have the option of not accepting a cell phone call if you know that you'll be merging onto a busy highway or making a turn at an intersection. In bad weather you have the option of being late for an appointment rather than getting into an accident. (You also have the option of checking the weather forecast to see if you should leave early, if possible, so that you can arrive safely AND on time). The problem with weighing all of your options in a driving situation is that many times you only have a couple seconds or less to make a decision. But I think that the more you keep your mind open to all possible options, the better and quicker you become at making decisions. You should make safety the top priority when making any decision. Good judgment is the underlying thought process that runs through every part of your job, from pre trip inspection to maneuvering your truck on the road.

Some of the suggestions in this book are just common courtesies, not traffic laws. You can spend your day trying to make up every possible second of your time, or you can back off now and then to save yourself some stress. For example, if you're on the highway and your exit is coming up you can make up a second or two by trying to get ahead of some vehicles up ahead, or you can get behind them and take your turn. It can take hours at the end of the day to recover from stress built up from trying to make up a few seconds here and there. It's not worth the few minutes that you've gained. Racing around all week to be home for two days can defeat the purpose if it takes a day to recover. It's better to get home a couple hours later and be able to enjoy your time there. Just remember that much of the stress on this job can be controlled by your attitude.

9

Unloading

OK, now you've made your way to your delivery. At this point your job is determined by what company you are employed by and what their customers require. You may get to your stop, hand them your paperwork, and they say, "Wait in your truck and we'll let you know when we're done". This is called "no touch freight". Or your company may have you back your trailer up to a dock, drop the trailer, hook up to another trailer and be on your way. You may have to assist in unloading your trailer, or perhaps you are the only one doing the unloading. It all depends on the job description for your company.

If you have a delivery route where you have to unload or wait to be unloaded, you might find that it's a good idea to call ahead. Some companies like to be notified a day before the delivery. If they have to make room on the dock for whatever you're bringing, it gives them some time to do it before you get there. It also helps them to arrange their schedule. They may have someone take an early lunch if they know you are on the way or they may keep someone there to help out instead of sending them on a delivery. Little things like this can save you time.

You have to use extra caution when entering a customer's loading area. Don't walk in with blinders on. There may be fork trucks coming down the aisles or around corners and the operators won't be expecting to see you standing there. If you need to help direct a fork truck driver to pick up something in your trailer, don't stand between the load that they are picking up and the inside wall of your trailer. Be careful when standing near a fork truck. I was talking to a fork truck operator once that was about to enter my trailer and I didn't realize that my foot was in front of the front wheel. It was my fault, not his. The tires on most fork trucks are made out of solid rubber, not the soft air filled tires like you find on a car. As he began moving forward, I felt the front tire up against the side of my foot and immediately felt my foot get hot from the pressure. Before it went over the top of my foot I yelled to the driver and he backed up. Luckily there was no damage done.

Be careful when walking near the edge of loading docks when entering or exiting your trailer. A driver that I worked with at one company accidentally stepped through an open section of a dock near the back of his trailer. On the way down he struck his face on a pipe sticking out of the ground. I rode along with my boss to pick up his truck while my boss picked him up from the hospital.

Just a quick word on making deliveries to Canada. The paperwork involved has been improved since companies started using bar codes on the paperwork. If everything goes as planned, the customs person scans it and you're on your way. But it won't help if they haven't been notified. Call your company and have them check that the broker and customs agents have been notified about your shipment. If you think that you're being a pain in the neck, just remember that it will be you who has to park the truck and walk down the street to find the broker's office and wait while everything gets straightened out. Once you are at your delivery, if a customer in Canada refuses something, or asks you to return something, call your company. You won't be allowed back across the border without paperwork for whatever is in your truck.

If you have a job like mine where you are physically unloading the trailer, pace yourself so that you don't wear yourself out before the job is done. Make sure that you eat enough food so that you'll have enough energy to unload your truck. I deliver a product that requires no particular temperature control (tires).The warehouses may be unheated in the winter and boiling hot in the summer so be ready to have the right clothing to wear.

I have a couple customer locations where I'm able to pull around a building to exit after unloading, but there are times in the winter when I can't swing around it because of snow banks. In those cases I have to back out into the street. Don't feel bad about asking one of the employees to watch for traffic as you back out. It's the smart thing to do. It lets you concentrate on turning at the best possible angle while not having to worry about traffic or pedestrians. After you're done unloading just say to one of the people, " I'm going to need some help backing out". Usually they're more than willing to help. Let them know which way you are going to point the rear of the trailer when backing into the street. An experienced driver doesn't feel bad about asking for help in this situation. They realize that it's the safest way to do this and that it's part of the job to do any maneuver in the safest way possible. This next diagram shows backing a trailer towards the passenger side into the street, so that you can exit towards the left down the street. Have the spotter stand in the street off to the driver side so that you'll be able to see him in your driver side mirror. If he's on the right side you'll lose sight of him as soon as you swing the tractor around. The trick is to back up so that you're close to the car on the right. This will give you the most room possible to complete the turn. If you think about it, if you had entered the parking lot coming from the right, this is about the same position your truck would be when entering. You're just reversing the process. While backing up, alternately watch the spotter plus the curb and left rear corner of the car until the trailer tandems are even with them. Once the tandems pass the car and the curb, the trailer will turn away from them when you turn the wheel to the left and angle the trailer into the street. Don't forget to check the cars parked on the left, because your tractor will be getting close to them when you turn the wheel to the right to follow the trailer into the street. To exit in the other direction, just reverse this process. Keep your trailer to the left and the spotter on the right.

Backing into a street

Watch the spotter in your left hand mirror and the car and curb in your right hand mirror. Keep the right corner of the trailer close to the right edge of the entrance. When your trailer tires go by the curb you can cut the wheel hard to the left to angle the trailer towards the right into the street. As soon as the trailer is on an angle to go into the middle of the street turn the wheel to the right to follow the trailer into the street.

spotter

10

Delivery Examples

I thought it might be helpful to show some of the deliveries that I make on my job and how I get around some of the obstacles. Most of my time driving a truck has been that of a peddle driver, delivering a product to retail stores or warehouses. But even if you work as a shuttle driver, delivering trailers to warehouses, the more you know about maneuvering in tight situations the better. These are real world examples of delivery locations and I hope that by going over this you can get some ideas about dealing with any situations that you may encounter on your job.

On this delivery I usually have plenty of room to back in (I have to be at dock #1). I pull up to the left curb (4 way flashers on), then pull ahead until the trailer is about 1/2 or 3/4 of the way in front of dock #1. Then I just turn the wheel about a 1/2 or 3/4 turn to the right to pull out at a gradual angle. I finish the set up at the angle you see in the diagram and turn the tractor slightly to the left so I can see the back of the trailer. On the right is a wall and a set of steps. Once I'm in straight I can see the steps but until then they're in my blind spot. If you go to the same location often, look for markings or little landmarks to help you. In this case there's a seam between the concrete pavement slabs. I know that as I'm backing up, if I keep the driver side rear corner of the trailer on the seam or close to it the trailer will be far enough away from the steps to avoid hitting them. When you're centered at the dock you're only a couple inches from the steps. I'm not too concerned about getting the first back up perfect. I'd rather be off center to the left instead of hitting the steps. Then after the tractor comes around and I can see out the right mirror, I do one or two pull ups to get close to the steps and centered at the dock.

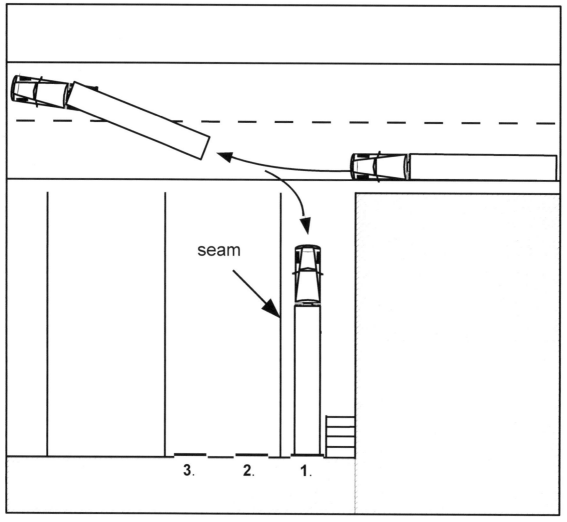

Use any space possible to make your back up easier. In this case I have to approach this delivery with the entrance on my right. I use their parking lot to swing out in the street going in the other direction so that the back up will be on my see side (driver side) making a better line of sight out of my driver side window and driver side mirror.

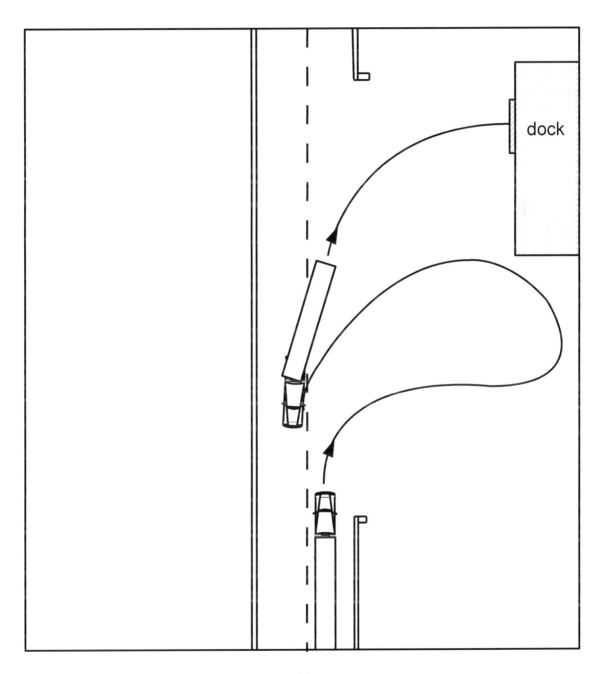

At this location I have to approach from the right. I could angle out in the street and do a blind side back up but the traffic here is usually very heavy. I pull into the lot, go around and between rows of parked cars, and then do a see side back up in the parking lot.

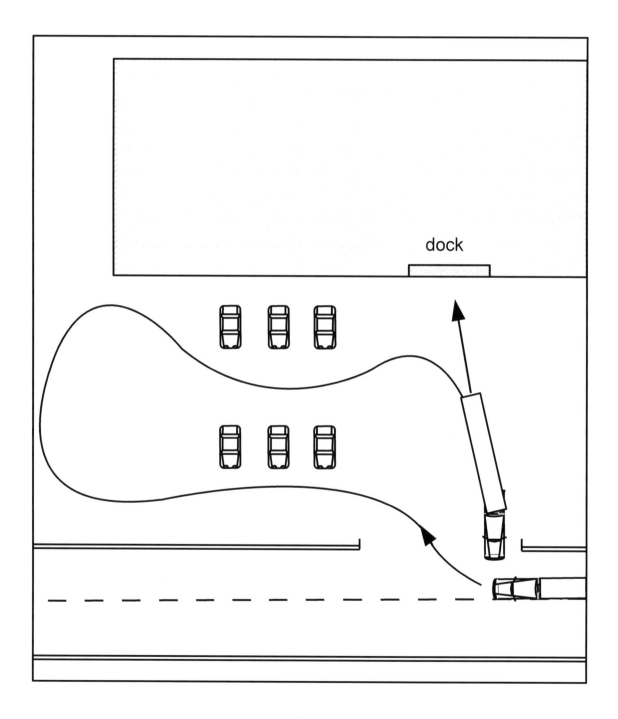

dock

Delivery Examples

Believe it or not this is a real delivery situation that I have in Herkimer, NY. The driveway at the bottom of the page is the only way in and out. Because of obstructions near the driveway entrance you can't turn around and back in the driveway. You have to drive in and then turn around. Again, in order to keep the rear of the trailer close to where it has to go I keep left when coming in then make a wide swing as close to the corner of the building as possible. There are three moves before you can back up to the dock.

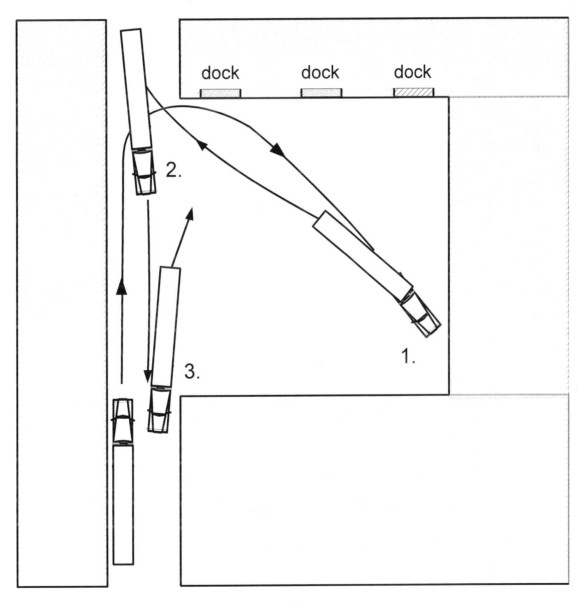

At this delivery I have to get around a building with very little room for the truck. I've mentioned getting the trailer close to an entrance or wherever you have to park it. Getting around something is just the opposite. You have to get the trailer as far away as possible. After pulling in I move the trailer to the right (like parallel parking). There's a curb too high to drive over but low enough for the rear overhang to clear. So I'm able to move the tandems forward (to make it easier in tight turns) and not worry about the rear swing of the trailer.

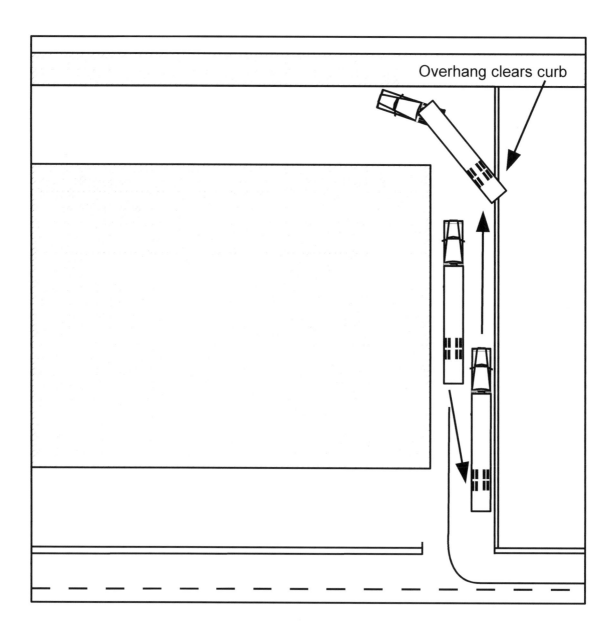

Overhang clears curb

This is the same delivery. After angling up to a loading door at the back side of the building the only way out is an alley between the buildings. Once again I have to keep the trailer away from the building that I'm trying to get around so I parallel park close to the wall (but not so close that the rear of the trailer will swing up against the wall). Then I can make the turn into the alley.

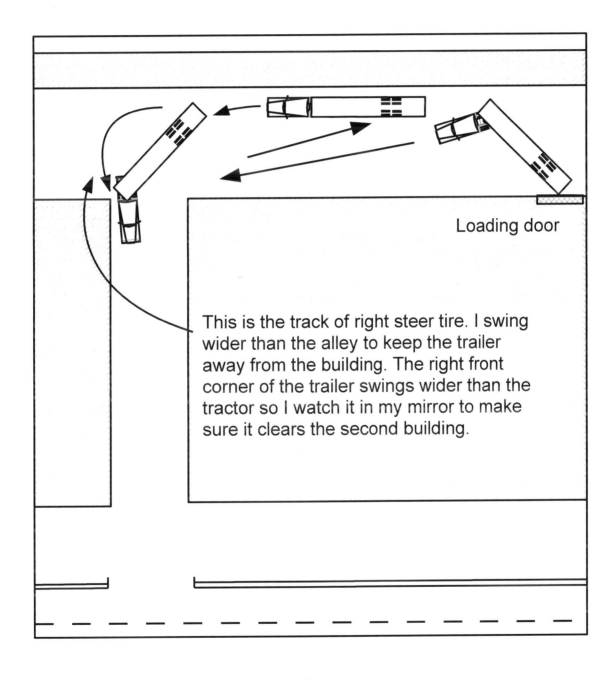

Loading door

This is the track of right steer tire. I swing wider than the alley to keep the trailer away from the building. The right front corner of the trailer swings wider than the tractor so I watch it in my mirror to make sure it clears the second building.

At this location I have to get around a building then make a sharp right turn to get on the street. The line is the path of my tractor. Remember to turn wide when going around obstacles because your trailer will be turning closer to that obstacle. After going around the building I steer wide to the left so the trailer clears the right curb of the entrance.

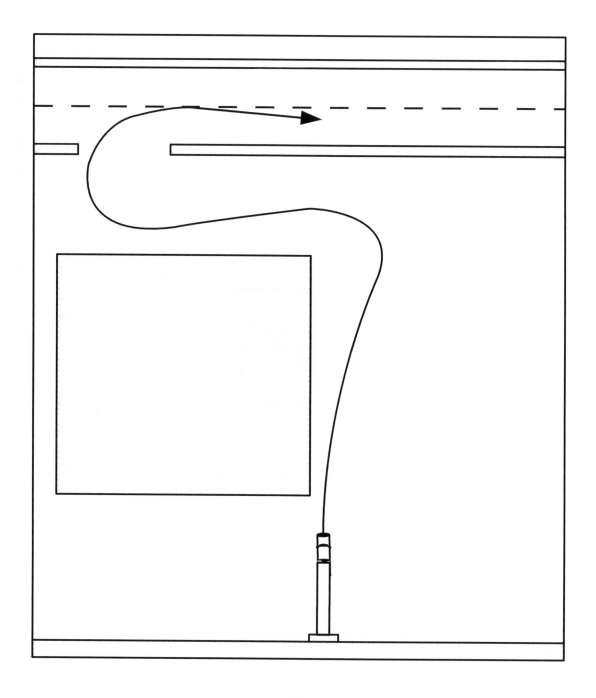

Here's a delivery near an intersection that shows another example of the importance of getting the rear of the trailer close to an entrance. Luckily I can usually get here early, before there's much traffic. But if there's someone on the right waiting for the light to turn green sometimes I wait for them to get a green light so they're out of my way, then I make a right on red if traffic allows it.

I turn as wide as possible, then hug the left curb with my left steer tire before turning out at an angle. This gets the rear of the trailer over as much as possible to make the back up into the entrance.

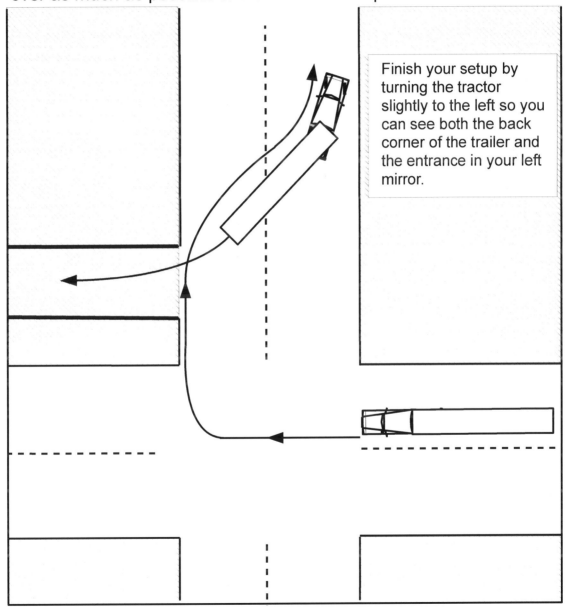

Finish your setup by turning the tractor slightly to the left so you can see both the back corner of the trailer and the entrance in your left mirror.

At this location I have to approach with the entrance on my right so I have to blind side in. I pull up to the right hand curb before the entrance and when traffic clears I angle out into the street far enough so that I can see the rear corner of the trailer in my right mirror as well as the right side of the entrance. I keep close to that right side of the entrance before angling in. There's a storage trailer sticking out before I get to the dock. So once I'm in the lot approaching the storage trailer I get out of the tractor to make sure it's clear on the other side of the storage trailer. Then I blind side in to the dock. It usually takes one or two pull ups to get straight to the dock.

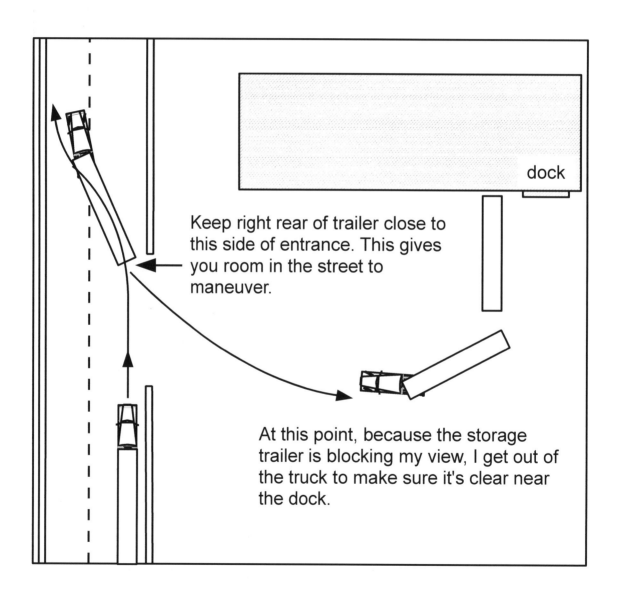

Keep right rear of trailer close to this side of entrance. This gives you room in the street to maneuver.

dock

At this point, because the storage trailer is blocking my view, I get out of the truck to make sure it's clear near the dock.

At this delivery, leaving the parking lot is harder than backing in. After I'm done I have to go around the building to get out. Again, this is just the opposite of the advice I've given about getting the rear of your trailer close to where it has to go. To get around something you need to get your trailer as far away from it as possible. After I'm done unloading I shift the trailer to the right (similar to parallel parking) to get around the building.

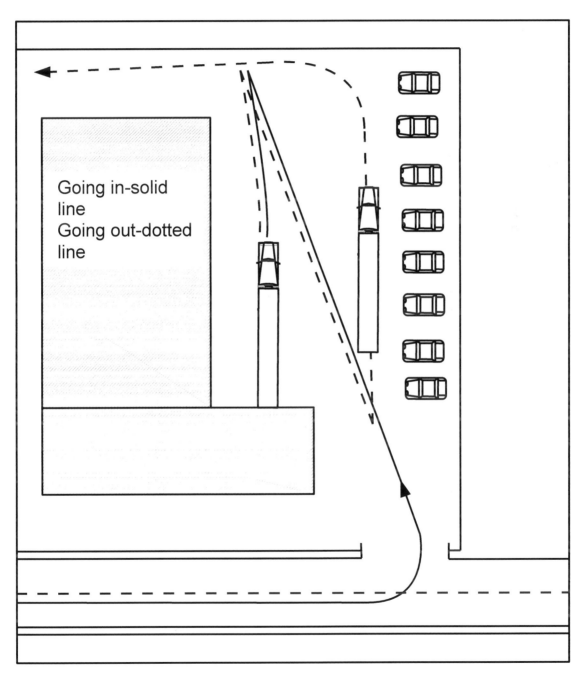

Going in-solid line
Going out-dotted line

11
Backing into a Truck Stop Parking Space

I've tried organizing this book into a typical work day: checking your vehicle, getting on a highway, a city street, then making a delivery. It would follow that in this last chapter there's a good chance that you'd be pulling into a truck stop at the end of your work day. Backing into a parking space at a truck stop has its own set of challenges.

Try to plan ahead to get an idea of where you want to be at the end of your work day if you're an over the road driver. Most truck stops sell directories showing truck stop locations across the country. You'll be able to judge how far you can get with the hours that you have available to see which truck stop you can reach by the end of the day. The directories give a description of each truck stop, including the size of the truck stop, whether they sell fuel, or have weigh scales, etc. Truck stops can vary a great deal. Some of the national chains have almost everything you need such as laundry, showers, barbershops, etc. Others are not much more than a dirt parking lot with pot holes that could swallow a car. As far as parking you usually find that the parking lots in the national chains have better lighting at night and there's more room to maneuver. That's why at the end of a work day I've often pulled up sooner than originally planned if it meant staying at one of the larger truck stops.

One advantage of parking at a truck stop is that, unlike a delivery where you might have cars and buildings in your way, you often have enough room to approach the parking space in a straight line in front of a row of trucks. If you've worked out a system of setting up your truck for this situation it can make the job a lot easier.

There may be no truck stops in the area where you'll be spending the night so be careful where you park. I used to deliver out to Long Island, N.Y. once every week or two. I found that it was much easier to go in on the night before my delivery and sleep in my truck at the warehouse parking lot rather than deal with New York city traffic in the morning. Or you may be able to find a rest area on the highway near your delivery. Many states have laws against parking on highway on and off ramps. If you can park on a highway ramp it's usually safer to use an on ramp rather than an off ramp. Traffic coming down an on ramp is usually going much slower than traffic coming onto an off ramp. If you're spending the night in a warehouse parking lot and you know that you'll be there for awhile the next day pick up some food and drinks before you get there.

Parking your truck at the end of the day can sometimes be the biggest challenge you'll face all day long. You may have to pull into a small truck stop that has narrow lanes between the rows of trucks. The yard where I drop my trailer every day consists of rows of dropped trailers with driving lanes that are fairly narrow, 55-60 ft., such as you might find at a small truck stop. With lanes this narrow, obviously you can't fit between the lanes in front of the space without first getting some of the trailer into the space. So your setup is crucial in a small parking lot. The spaces in my lot are 12 feet wide. That leaves between 3 and 4 feet between the trailers, and even less, when you consider how far the mirrors stick out on the tractors. At a small truck stop you may only have a few inches of clearance between your mirrors and the mirrors on the trucks next to you. Sometimes when I'm faced with a difficult backup at a dock or a truck stop I tell myself that there is a perfect line to follow. A line, if I could only find it, that would put the tractor and trailer squarely into the middle of the space the first time without having to pull up and make any adjustments. Of course, I'll usually have to pull up at least once to get the truck centered. You've probably noticed, as I have, that it's much easier pulling OUT of a parking space than it is backing IN to a space. So it follows that the line that you take pulling out of a space has got to be close to the perfect line for backing into the space. I experimented with this in some empty parking lots and at the yard where I drop my trailer.

I started by pulling out of a space and then turning the wheel over hard to the left when I could see that the rear of my trailer would clear the one next to mine. Then I straightened out at the last minute so that my truck would end up in a straight line and at a 90 degree angle to the trailers (see diagram below). I would have thought that I'd end up in different spots depending on the length of the trailer, but whether it was a 45, 48, or 53 foot trailer, the end of the trailer ended up roughly 12 feet away from the row and the rear of the trailer was about a space and a half or 18 feet past the space. Of course, the tractor was further down the line when I used a longer trailer. So now, I know that if I pull up 12 feet from the row with the rear of the trailer a space and a half past my target space, I just need to reverse my steering pattern to get into the space. The only problem is that it's difficult to see the distance from the rear of the trailer to the parking space when you're sitting in the cab. If you want to try this method, one thing you can do is to angle slightly out to the right after going about 4 spaces past your target space and then angle a little to the left for a couple more spaces, so that you can see the back of the trailer.

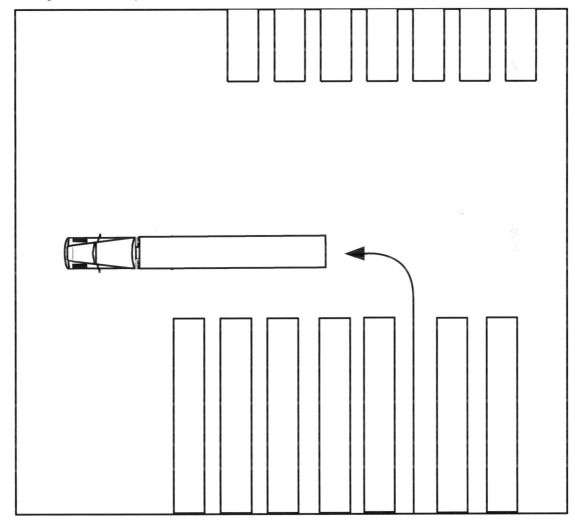

Or you can do what you'll see most drivers do when they park at a truck stop, that is driving along the row and then angling out before backing up. This is similar to the 4 step setup shown on page 65, but I found that in a small lot I wasn't able to get the tractor completely parallel to the row as in step 2, and I also found that I had to start angling out further down the line. I also wanted a more precise way of measuring when to start angling out, so instead of using the drive wheels as a guide, I used the rear post on my driver side window (easier to see from where you're sitting). Using a 48 foot trailer, I found that it was best to approach about 12 feet away from the row and start angling out when my window post was just past the beginning of the second space past my target space. I cut the wheel hard to the right until the trailer was about 45 degrees to the parking spot. In the case of a small lot like this I angle to the right until I get close to the trucks or trailers in the opposite row. Then I turn the wheel to the left, continue about the length of the tractor, and finish with the tractor at a 90 degree angle to the row as in step 3 on page 65. Now I was set up to back in. Using a 53 foot trailer in a small parking lot I found it was better to make the first approach about 8 feet (about the width of a trailer) in front of the row.

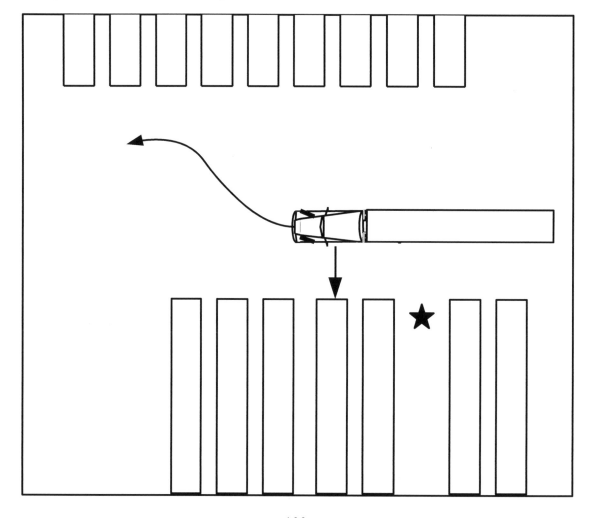

Updated Version

On the next two pages I describe an updated version of this set up. This is in response to requests from some new drivers who wanted to see exact turns of the steering wheel in this backing description. I use whole numbers for the steering wheel turns (easier to remember). Also, instead of turning out at the second space past the target space I'm turning out at the target space (also easier to remember).

I've mentioned that there are many things that can affect your back up. They include:

The wheel base of your tractor

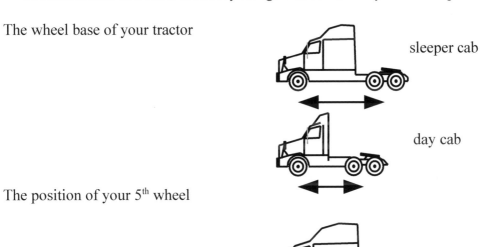

sleeper cab

day cab

The position of your 5th wheel

The length of your trailer and position of your tandems

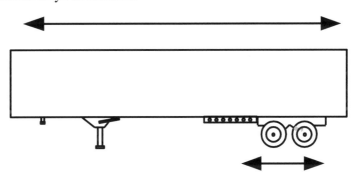

45 degree back up into a parking space

1. Approach with approximately 8 feet of space (the width of a trailer) in front of the row of trucks or trailers.
2. When your window post (at your left shoulder) passes by the end of the open space (see diagram on next page) turn the wheel one full turn to the right and angle out to the right, keeping the wheel at that one turn.
3. If you're at a small lot like I was (lanes approximately 60 feet wide) continue until you get close to the opposite row then turn the wheel approximately 3 full turns to the left and continue for about the length of the tractor. If there are no vehicles in a row opposite of yours, figure on angling out for about 50 feet before making that left turn with your tractor.
4. Before coming to a stop, turn the wheel 2 full turns to the right to make the tractor face perpendicular to the row that you're backing into (see tractor in upper part of diagram).
5. If you add up the turns of the wheel (total of 3 to the right and 3 to the left) it puts the steering wheel back straight in the original position. So now you're set up with the tractor and trailer at an angle to each other with the steer tires straight.
6. Your set up is complete as shown in the diagram. Because the tractor and trailer are at an angle to each other, when you start backing with the steer tires straight the trailer automatically starts turning towards the left. So at this point, when you start to back up, you may have to immediately start turning gradually to the left if it looks as though the trailer is turning too sharply, or keep the wheels straight if you need to make the trailer turn sharper.

As shown on the previous page, there are many factors such as your tractor wheel base and trailer tandems that affect your back up. You'll need to experiment with this back up. If your set up doesn't leave your trailer pointing to the space I would keep the turns of the wheel the same but experiment with where you make your first turn out. For instance, if you have a short wheel base tractor or short trailer and find yourself pointing towards trailer A, next time try making your turn out earlier, when you pass the beginning of the parking space. With a long wheel base tractor and long trailer if you end up pointing towards trailer B, next time try turning out a few feet past the end of the parking space. If you have the same tractor and trailer every day you should be able to work out the same set up that you can use every time for this kind of back up.

45 degree back up into a parking space

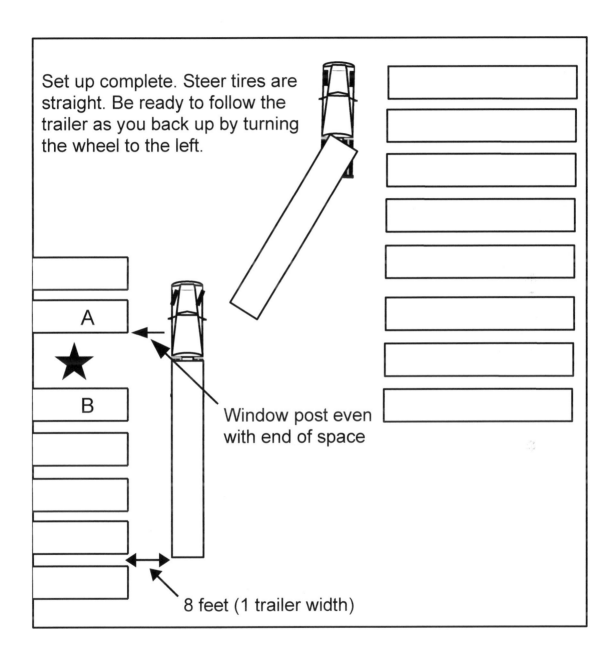

Set up complete. Steer tires are straight. Be ready to follow the trailer as you back up by turning the wheel to the left.

A

B

Window post even with end of space

8 feet (1 trailer width)

Correcting a 45 degree back up

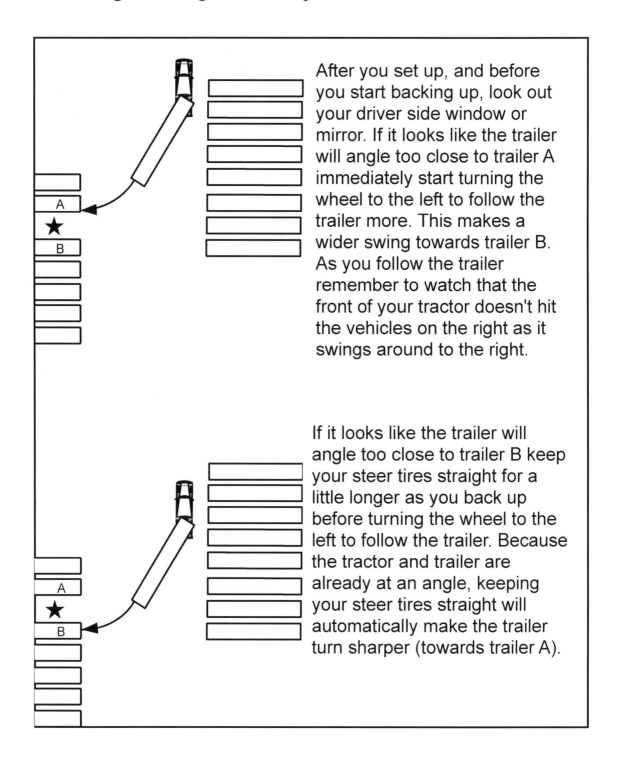

After you set up, and before you start backing up, look out your driver side window or mirror. If it looks like the trailer will angle too close to trailer A immediately start turning the wheel to the left to follow the trailer more. This makes a wider swing towards trailer B. As you follow the trailer remember to watch that the front of your tractor doesn't hit the vehicles on the right as it swings around to the right.

If it looks like the trailer will angle too close to trailer B keep your steer tires straight for a little longer as you back up before turning the wheel to the left to follow the trailer. Because the tractor and trailer are already at an angle, keeping your steer tires straight will automatically make the trailer turn sharper (towards trailer A).

Backing into a Truck Stop Parking Space

Even at a truck stop you won't always be able to make a straight approach along a line of trucks. An example would be trying to park in a space near the end of a row after coming around a corner. You won't be getting out of your truck to pace off the distance to a parking space but if you know how the trailer should look in relation to the space under ideal conditions you can try to reproduce that look when coming in at a different angle.

At the end of the day I do my walk around to check for any problems on the tractor or trailer in the same order that I do in the morning. As I said earlier, I think this helps to prevent you from overlooking anything. If you or someone else has fueled your truck, double check that the fuel caps are on and that the hood latches are fastened if you've had the hood up to check the oil. As you do your post trip inspection, check the instrument gauges one last time. You want to make sure that everything is working before you get in it again or before handing it off to someone else. Many companies have 24 hour repair services that can repair your truck between the time that you shut it down and the time that it has to go out again as long as you take the time to make the phone call and arrange the repairs. It may seem to be no big deal if a couple marker lights aren't working on the trailer. But if you're stopped because of an emergency on the highway and traffic is coming behind you over the top of a hill, the first thing that they should see are the top marker lights on your trailer. Many serious accidents are caused by small details that aren't taken care of properly.

You've probably been taught this, but whenever you need to unhook and drop the trailer it's much easier if you've taken pressure off of the kingpin, making it easier to pull the release handle. To do this first park the trailer where you want it, then pull the red trailer brake button to set only the trailer brakes. Then, when you have the tractor in reverse, slightly back off on the clutch until you feel the tractor back up against the kingpin. While you have it pushing up against the kingpin, pull the yellow parking brake button to set the tractor brakes, depress the clutch, then put the tractor in neutral. This takes the pressure off of the sliding mechanism of the 5th wheel making it much easier to pull the release handle.

I hope that I've given you at least a couple suggestions in this book that you can use on your job. Good luck and be safe.

Made in the USA
Middletown, DE
08 August 2019